CW00674597

THE DIVINER'S HANDBOOK
EXPLORING MAGIK DIVINATION TECHNIQUES

DAVID THOMPSON

THE DIVINER'S HANDBOOK
EXPLORING MAGIK DIVINATION TECHNIQUES

DAVID THOMPSON
HIGH MAGIK BOOK 10

Copyright © 2023 David Thompson

All rights reserved.

ISBN: 978-1-961765-12-2

No part of this book may be reproduced, or stored in a retrieval system, or transmitted in any form or by any means, electronic, mechanical, photocopying, recording, or otherwise, without express written permission of the publisher.

Cover Image: ID 26466951 © Nataliia Dubchak | Dreamstime.com

Cover design by: David Thompson

Please note - this book is filled by weight, not volume. Some settling may have occurred during shipment and handling.

To Apollo, God of Divination

Introduction

So, what is Divination?

As defined by the Oxford English Dictionary, it is:

"The action or practice of divining; the foretelling of future events or discovery of what is hidden or obscure by supernatural or magical means…"

Supernatural or magical means.

This means this information has come to you outside the normal channels of gathering information - the physical world. Yeah. Fine. But in all seriousness, divination is not magik, nor is it supernatural. It relies on the fact that most everyone is, to some degree, psychic, whether or not they believe in it. Popular, "Brand Name" religions rely upon supernatural texts to educate (indoctrinate) their followers. The so-called "supernatural" is all around us. We just tend to ignore it, as human tend to do when encountering something that is beyond the scope of our human minds.

And divination can scare people. It freaks them out, often due to their religious affiliation. Divination, like tarot or astrology, is linked in their minds to so-called "Satanic" forces. However, for me, these are just tools. Tools needed to help me practice so-called "magik". In my mind, hidden somewhere in the back, probably behind an unused metal filing cabinet, lurking alongside ideas for some unwritten novels and it's possibly sitting alongside a long-forgotten school locker combination, is my idea that magik is actually a long-lost technology. It's just that being trapped in a decaying biological meat-bag, humans can only recognize technology that they can hold, play with, and in some cases, have sex with.

Humans can't recognize how mental abilities, such as telepathy or "ESP" are just technologies that exist in a non-physical realm.

But this is a type of technology.

And, in that case, this is less an "occult book" and more of a reference manual using definitions unique to me and my view of various methods of fathoming out the future, or why some magik rituals failed to work, or gaining some insight about any odd dreams I might have had the previous night.

Hang on. This is a lengthy book. Not my longest book, that title goes to my "Furies" novels.

Also, have fun with this.

Chapter One

How to read this book.

Hey, you're doing pretty good thus far – so keep it up*![1]

About this here book.

This particular book is an experiment, honestly. What would happen if I condensed decades of working with tarot, pendulum, other divination methods and wrote it all into a book. Then, I decided to incorporate three books into this one book.

This book actually incorporates the highlights of all

---

[1] Honestly, I've wanted to put this in a book, after having spotted an index entry labeled that a few years ago, in one of those annoying pop-ads on social media trying to sell a book about selling books.

the books I'd read through my 20s and 30s on divination, including my fitful attempts to distill decades of interpreting the tarot into a middle section of this book. I tried to cover all the methods I've used, but the major aspects of Divination I cover are the Pendulum, Tarot, and Astrology. Then a chapter on the other forms I have experiments with over the past half-century.

This book is a reference manual. It's a collection of my brain-droppings from over the past half-century, while I played with the various methods of fathoming out my own future, learning what works, what doesn't, and then making myself write down each and every divination session in a notebook.

I can't go into too much detail in each section, as then this book would be considerably longer. However, I hope the reference sections will help you in gaining an understanding of the various divination methods one can use to help make sense of this weird thing we call life.

Divination – a quick method of figuring out WHY sometimes magik will simply not work. I have received direct messages, via pendulum or tarot, from spirits I had petitioned why a specific ritual failed.

It also helps to understand messages from spirits, and to see if an unexpected event is part of the magik working.

Divination is handy, and I kinda figure it's something ya'll need to know.

This is something that has always fascinated me, and in my 20s I was reading book after book on divination methods, I must have had an entire book shelf on divination, tarot, crystal balls, and the like.

If you have the knowledge of how to read cards, use a pendulum, or cast an astrology chart, it can be a huge assistance in achieving successful magik. The reason I can only cover some topics in divination within this book is that I don't want it to be over 500 pages long. So, I limit the topics to tarot, astrology, the pendulum, plus a chapter on the other divination methods I have personally tried.

In most cases, I'll present the information I have collected across decades of working with these methods, plus some generally available Tarot and astrological interpretations (say, found online). For example, I'll include the more traditional interpretation of the tarot, and with each card, I'll follow that up by what I have learned it often means *for me*. As you learn, make notes, you will also begin to know what the cards mean *for you*! It's a very personal process.

My history with the Tarot begins when I was in college, and a girlfriend insisted we get some tarot cards. So, we bought the most popular cards in the world – the

Rider Deck. Then that paperback book to interpret the cards. The one in the black cover. Man, that book gave me the gloomiest of outcomes, but – and this is the fascinating part – it proved to be quite accurate. I mean, I'd shuffle and reshuffle, like that meme on social media, "That Bitch, you'd better reshuffle!" meme. You know that one. Or, go google it. Even after the third or fourth shuffling and layout, the damned cards kept saying the same thing - and that would be the eventual outcome!

So, from there on out, I was hooked on divination. I was constantly buying books, learning new methods, and expanding out to experiment with I-Ching, the Pendulum, regular playing cards, and even unsuccessful attempts with crystal balls and black mirrors. I skipped the reading of the entrails of birds and farm animals.

As you'll read later, I also did a deep dive into astrology. I mean, this was before the proliferation of computer programs to help you cast a chart, so I had books and books piled on my desk while I crafted a horoscope for myself and my then wife. More on this in the chapter on Astrology.

I admit, I had a hard time working on the scrying chapters. That's because no matter how hard I try, I just can't seem to 'click" and begin seeing visions. When my kid was 6-ish I bought a large six-inch crystal ball on eBay. It was a prop for a photo shoot, but I decided to learn to use it, as it was real crystal. Nothing. No matter what I did, it just didn't work.

My daughter sat down with it, and asked, "All I see are snowflakes..." which, as you'll read, is the signal that you are getting it to work. Sigh.

I also have a chapter on my all-time favorite divination method, the pendulum. I've included its use in my magik books as a way to communicate with the summoned spirit, for fast yes/no questions. In fact, it's the lead chapter on divination methods. I have had the same pendulum for close to thirty years. I found it when eBay was new and was easy to buy from individual artists. More in that chapter.

Okay, that's all for the introduction. Have fun reading, watch for my subtle jokes, and hopefully, you'll broaden your horizons in using divination!

Chapter Two

The History and Importance of Divination

Divination has had a major role in high magic throughout history. Its roots can be traced back to ancient civilizations, where it was embraced to gain insight into the unknown and connecting with the divine. In this section, we will explore the fascinating history and enduring importance of divination practices, catering specifically to high magic students with niches in tarot card reading and interpretation, astrology and horoscope analysis, as well as various divination techniques and practices like scrying and pendulum dowsing. I'll be skipping the odder methods of divination, such as reading the entrails of a sheep or fathoming the messages of spirits using bones.

Essentially, the practice of divination involves seeking knowledge or guidance from a supernatural source, which is considered an art. Divination, which is the practice of foretelling the future or seeking knowledge through supernatural means, has a long and rich history that can be traced back thousands of years to the ancient civilizations of Mesopotamia, Egypt, and China. The people of these civilizations believed that through divination, they could connect with gods and spirits, and as a result, gain insight into their lives and the world they lived in, allowing them to make informed decisions.

The use of tarot cards for divination started in the late 14th century, when people began using playing cards to interpret the future. Over time, the Tarot deck changed and became a powerful tool for self-reflection, giving deep insights about your past, present, and future. Nowadays, tarot card reading is super popular. It guides people towards clarity on love, career, and personal growth.

Astrology and horoscope analysis have their origins in ancient civilizations, such as Babylonia and Egypt. The study of celestial bodies and their influence on human affairs has been a central tenet of astrology throughout history. By analyzing the positions of stars and planets at the time of an individual's birth, astrologers can provide valuable insights into their personality traits, life events, and potential paths to success.

Tarot and astrology are not the only divination

techniques and practices that have been around for centuries; in fact, there are many others. One example of divination is scrying, which requires a person to focus their gaze on reflective surfaces, such as water or mirrors, with the aim of receiving visions or symbolic images. (A method I find very challenging, honestly. Which is why I rarely resort to scrying.) While other methods of divination require specific tools, such as tarot cards or crystal balls, pendulum dowsing uses a simple yet effective technique by suspending a weighted object from a chain or string to answer yes or no questions. Diviners all over the world have made use of these practices, with each diviner offering their own unique approach to seeking answers from the unseen realms.

The significance of divination cannot be overstated, as it possesses the potential to offer valuable guidance and direction in a world that is teeming with uncertainties. Divination practitioners have the capability of tapping into the great reservoir of ancient wisdom and establishing a connection with the spiritual realm, thus gaining valuable insights that can help them overcome life's obstacles and make informed choices. Divination is a valuable tool in today's world, where rationality is often the dominant force, because it helps to remind us that there is more to the universe than what we can see with our eyes.

For students of high magic, who have a keen interest

in tarot card reading, astrology, and various other divination techniques, it is crucial to have a deep understanding of the history and significance of divination. Through the study and exploration of these ancient practices, individuals can develop a deeper understanding and connection with the mysterious energies that shape our existence, which ultimately empowers them to improve their lives and create a brighter future.

The Role of Divination in High Magic

Using divination, which is an integral part of high magic, presents us with an opportunity to unravel the mysteries of the universe and attain a comprehension of the elusive energies that steer the trajectory of our existence. Regardless of your level of expertise in high magic, it is crucial to comprehend the importance and potency of divination if you wish to advance on your individual path. By working a divination prior to a ritual, you can then check easily enough how the magik may have altered the energy surrounding the energy of your ritual purpose. I have used the pendulum to test which spirit I should use for a ritual, often just a series of yes/no questions.

Such as "Is Lilith right for this desire? Yes/no." "Is Apollo nearby and willing to work with me? Yes/No." "Is my guide Daniel tired of me asking all the questions? YES I

AM!! Now stop!'"

The pendulum continues to be my preferred method of divination, whether during a ritual or afterwards. During a ritual, if I feel I am having difficulty hearing the spirit, I will grab my pendulum and begin to ask yes/no questions. At first, it may appear nonsensical to ask only yes/no questions, but the pendulum is the best way to a clean yes or no answer. By asking multiple questions, using only a yes/no chart (more on that later), you can quickly figure out what may be happening if your magik appears to have failed.

Tarot card reading and interpretation are among the most popular forms of divination, allowing practitioners to tap into the universal energies and gain valuable guidance. Each card in the Tarot deck represents a unique aspect of life, and through careful interpretation, the reader can unveil hidden truths and potential paths. By understanding the symbolism and meanings of the cards, the practitioner can navigate life's twists and turns with clarity and confidence.

Tarot card readings have been around for centuries and have been used by people from all walks of life to gain insight into different aspects of their lives. The cards themselves are rich in symbolism and meaning, with each one representing a different archetype or energy. This makes the Tarot a powerful tool for self-discovery and personal growth. Tarot readings are often sought when people are facing difficult decisions or are feeling lost or uncertain about the future. The cards can provide clarity and guidance, helping people to make more informed choices and navigate their lives with greater ease. The process of a Tarot reading can vary depending on the practitioner and the client's needs. Some readers may use a specific spread or layout of cards, while others may simply draw cards one at a time and interpret their meanings at the moment. I personally never read a card in its reversed position, because I find that unnecessarily pessimistic.

Regardless of the approach, the goal of a Tarot reading is always to help the client gain a deeper understanding of themselves and their circumstances. It is not about predicting the future but rather about empowering the reader to make the best possible choices for themselves based on the information provided by the cards. Overall, Tarot card reading and interpretation are valuable tools for anyone looking to gain insight into their lives and make more informed decisions. With the right practitioner and an open mind, a Tarot reading can be a powerful and transformative experience.

Astrology is a field of study that involves analyzing the positions and movements of celestial bodies in order to gain insight into how they affect our lives and shape our destinies, while horoscope analysis is a related practice that involves interpreting the astrological information that is specific to each individual based on their date and time of birth. Astrologers are able to determine the energies that impact our lives by studying the positions and movements of celestial bodies. By providing a snapshot of the heavens at the precise moment of our birth, the birth chart offers a blueprint of our personality traits, strengths, weaknesses, and potential life events. By studying astrology and practicing high magic, students are able to gain a profound insight into their personal identity and their role within the vast universe.

There are various divination techniques that can be used to tap into the hidden realms, such as scrying and pendulum dowsing. The ancient art of scrying involves gazing into a reflective surface, such as a crystal ball or mirror, which can transport practitioners into a meditative state that enables them to receive messages and visions from beyond our world. The process of pendulum dowsing entails suspending a weighted object on a string and utilizing it to provide responses to yes or no inquiries. Through the utilization of their intuitive abilities and establishing a connection with the spiritual realm, students of high magik can actively seek guidance and obtain a deeper understanding of their current circumstances as well as their future.

It is important to keep in mind that divination, while useful, should not be relied on as an absolute predictor of the future. Rather than a mere tool, it functions as a compass, providing invaluable guidance and illuminating potential outcomes. It empowers practitioners to make informed choices, navigate challenges, and harness their own innate power to shape their lives.

The trajectory of the energy surrounding an issue will shift after working a successful ritual. By using divination to see the shift, this helps assure you, the high magik student, that your magik is actually working.

The growth and development of magik practitioners largely depends on their study and practice of divination techniques and practices, as they are crucial to their spiritual advancement. If you take the time to hone your skills and gain a deep understanding of the role of divination in high magic, you will be able to unlock the secrets of the universe and set out on a transformative journey towards self-discovery and empowerment.

Chapter Three

Pendulum Dowsing: Seeking Answers

So, here we go, y'all! My favorite in-ritual divination technique.

For those of you who are already immersed in the niches of tarot card reading and interpretation, astrology and horoscope analysis, and other divination techniques, pendulum dowsing offers a unique and complementary tool to enhance your mystical toolkit.

Pendulum dowsing is a divination practice that dates back centuries. It involves using a weighted object, often a crystal or metal pendant, attached to a chain or string. The pendulum acts as a conduit for accessing the subconscious mind and the collective unconscious, providing answers to questions that stir within us.

In this section, we'll start with the fundamentals of pendulum dowsing. We begin by understanding the importance of setting intentions and creating a sacred space for divination. I'll then guide you through the process of choosing the perfect pendulum for your personal energy and needs, ensuring a strong connection between you and the tool.

Once you have found your ideal pendulum, I'll delve into the various techniques and methods of pendulum dowsing. From simple yes/no responses to more complex queries, you will learn how to effectively communicate with the pendulum and interpret its movements.

I'll address the significance of calibration and cleansing rituals to maintain the purity of your pendulum's energy. I'll provide you with practical exercises to strengthen your energetic connection with the pendulum. I'll also give you links (see the appendix) to the best pendulum dowsing chart I have ever encountered.

To enhance your understanding of pendulum dowsing, we will explore the potential applications of this technique. Whether you seek to gain insights about your personal life, unravel the mysteries of the universe, or delve into past lives, pendulum dowsing can assist you on your mystical journey.

Finally, we will discuss the ethics and responsibility that come with engaging in divination practices. As students of the occult and divination, it is crucial to approach these practices with respect, integrity, and a genuine desire to seek truth and guidance.

Choosing the Right Pendulum

Pendulum dowsing is a powerful divination technique that has been practiced for centuries. It involves using a weighted object, typically a crystal or metal pendulum, to gain insight and answers from the spiritual realm. As a high magic student, it is essential to choose the right pendulum that resonates with your energy and intentions. In this section, we will explore the various factors to consider when selecting a pendulum for your divination practices. Mine is a piece of amethyst, cut into a up-side-down pyramid, with a delicate silver chain. I've had mine since the early 1990s. It's never far from my altar, except when I need to get an answer while not in ritual.

The most important factor to consider when choosing a pendulum is how comfortable it feels in your hand, as this can greatly affect the accuracy of your readings. The weight and shape of the object are crucial factors to consider when choosing a pendulum to use during divination sessions, as it will be held for extended periods.

Take the time to hold different pendulums and determine which one feels the most natural and balanced.

Another vital aspect to consider is the material of the

pendulum. Different materials have varying energy properties, and you should select one that aligns with your intentions. For example, crystals like amethyst or clear quartz are known for their spiritual and healing properties, making them ideal for divination purposes. On the other hand, metals such as brass or silver can offer a more grounded and practical energy. Choose a material that resonates with the type of energy you wish to connect with during your divination practice.

Next, consider the shape and design of the pendulum. Some pendulums may have a pointed end, while others may be more rounded or even contain symbols or engravings. The shape can influence the way the pendulum swings and the energy it emits. Experiment with different shapes and designs to determine which one facilitates clearer communication with the spiritual realm.

Lastly, trust your intuition when choosing a pendulum. Allow yourself to be drawn to a particular pendulum, even if it doesn't conform to traditional guidelines. Your intuition is a powerful tool in the world of divination and can guide you towards the pendulum that is most attuned to your energy.

You can also make a pendulum. This is what I used to do before buying one. I took my college graduation ring, a nice, heavy lump of gold, then tied a length of twine to it, and started working with it. You can also use small chains and pendants, some people will make a pendulum out of a necklace, especially a crystal necklace.

Remember, the right pendulum is a personal choice, and what works for one person may not work for another. Trust your instincts, experiment with different options, and choose the pendulum that resonates with you on a deep level. By selecting the right pendulum, you will enhance your divination practices and open doors to the ancient wisdom and guidance that await you.

Cleansing and Energizing the Pendulum

Among the various divination techniques, the pendulum holds a special place in my heart as one such tool. For centuries, individuals have used this ancient tool to tap into the unseen energies and gaining valuable insights into what the future may hold. However, like any instrument, the pendulum requires regular cleansing and energizing to maintain its effectiveness.

Cleansing the pendulum is essential to remove any lingering energies that may have attached themselves to it during divination sessions. These energies can interfere with the accuracy of your readings and may cloud your intuitive abilities. If you have just acquired a pendulum, then it definitely needs to be cleansed. Even having it in a room where people often visit, the pendulum can still pick up stray energy. There are several methods you can employ to cleanse your pendulum, depending on your personal preferences and the materials you have at hand.

One popular method is to place the pendulum under running water, allowing the natural flow to wash away any unwanted energies. Don't do this with a pendulum made of any material that can be damaged by exposure to water. If you live close to a river or creek, it's a simple matter of dipping the pendulum into the water, and allowing it to flow over and around the pendulum. While doing this in the creek that ran behind my house in Texas, I also noticed how some fish were drawn to the pendulum. Just remember, the purpose here is to cleanse the pendulum, not catch dinner.

You can also immerse the pendulum in a bowl of saltwater, or a bowl or plastic bag of regular salt, or even bury it in the earth for a period to absorb the cleansing energies of the earth. (Just mark where you buried it.)

Energizing your pendulum after cleaning is needed, as this infuses the tool with your own personal energy and intention. To energize your pendulum, begin by holding it in your dominant hand and close your eyes, focusing on your breath. Visualize a bright golden/yellow light surrounding the pendulum, infusing it with positive energy and intention. You may choose to recite a simple affirmation or prayer, stating your intention for the pendulum to be a clear channel of divination and guidance.

Regularly cleansing and energizing your pendulum not only ensures its accuracy but also strengthens your connection to the divine energies that guide your practice. By taking the time to care for this sacred tool, you are honoring the ancient traditions of divination and cultivating a deeper understanding of yourself and the world around you.

Asking Questions and Interpreting the Pendulum's Movements

The incredible power of the pendulum can be harnessed to reveal the secrets of the universe that are hidden from view, and to gain insight into the answers to even the most pressing questions if you learn to use it correctly. The movements of your pendulum are influenced by both the energy of the universe and your subconscious mind, making it an extremely valuable tool in your quest for divination.

The pendulum is a simple tool, consisting of a weight suspended on a string or chain. However, when used correctly, it can provide profound insights into the mysteries of the universe. The pendulum works by tapping into the energy of the universe and your own subconscious mind, allowing you to access information that is normally hidden from view.

Learning to use the pendulum correctly takes practice and patience. It is important to approach it with an open mind and a willingness to learn. With time and practice, you can harness the incredible power of the pendulum to gain insight into the mysteries of the universe and unlock the answers to even the most pressing questions.

The aim of this section is to explore the art of asking questions effectively so that you can gain valuable insights and we will be doing that throughout this section. Planning your questions in a clear and concise manner is of utmost importance, as it guarantees accurate interpretations. In the following discussion, I will attempt to guide you through various types of questions that you can use. These questions will include open-ended ones that will help you gain broad insights, as well as closed-ended ones that will provide specific answers.

There are many intricacies to interpreting the pendulum's movements, and I will take the time to explore them thoroughly. Each direction and pattern holds a unique significance, and I'll provide you with a comprehensive guide on how to read and analyze these movements. Discover the difference between clockwise and counterclockwise rotations, vertical and horizontal swings, and the significance of the pendulum's stillness.

To enhance your understanding, I'll also address common challenges faced while interpreting pendulum movements. These challenges may include external influences, personal biases, or interpreting ambiguous movements. By being aware of these hurdles, you will be better equipped to navigate through them and attain accurate insights.

We will unravel the connection between the pendulum and your intuition. Trusting your instincts is crucial when working with divination tools, and the pendulum is no exception. Learn how to tap into your intuitive powers to enhance the accuracy of your interpretations and build a stronger connection with the pendulum's energy.

As high magic students, we understand the importance of practice and experimentation. Through hands-on exercises and real-life examples, we will empower you to develop your skills and deepen your understanding of the pendulum's language.

Calibrating and Finding the Best Posture for Using The Pendulum

Foremost, it is important to find a comfortable and relaxed position before using the pendulum. This ensures that your mind is clear and your body is in harmony with the energies surrounding you. Whether standing or sitting, make sure you are in a calm and focused state of mind.

When holding the pendulum, it is recommended to use your dominant hand. This hand is usually more attuned to your energy and will facilitate a stronger connection with the pendulum. Gently grasp the chain or string of the pendulum between your thumb and forefinger, allowing it to dangle freely.

Ensure that your grip is firm yet gentle, allowing the pendulum to swing naturally.

Positioning the pendulum is also important for accurate divination. One popular stance is to hold the pendulum directly above a flat surface, such as a table or a divination board.

This allows for clearer readings as the pendulum swings freely with no obstructions. Another technique is to hold the pendulum over a map or a diagram related to the specific question or topic you are divining about. This method can provide more detailed and specific answers.

Experimenting with different positions and stances can help you find what works best for you. Some practitioners find that standing with their feet shoulder-width apart enhances their connection with the pendulum, while others prefer to sit in a meditative position.

Trust your intuition and allow yourself to explore various stances until you feel a strong energetic connection.

As you work towards mastering the pendulum, it is important to keep in mind that practice and patience will be key factors in achieving your goal. With repeated use of this divinatory tool, you will gradually develop a deeper understanding of its unique language and symbolism that will ultimately help you interpret its messages more accurately. Once you have mastered the art of holding and positioning the pendulum, you will be able to unlock the secrets of the universe and gain invaluable insights that will allow you to delve deeper into the world of high magik.

It is important to remember that the pendulum is a tool, and like any tool, it requires practice and dedication to master. It may take time to develop a clear and consistent connection with the pendulum, but with patience and persistence, you will begin to see results.

In addition to finding a comfortable position and holding the pendulum correctly, it is also important to approach divination with a clear and focused mind. Take a few moments to clear your thoughts and set your intention before beginning a divination session. This will help you to better connect with the energies and vibrations that the pendulum responds to.

As you begin to use the pendulum more regularly,

you may also want to experiment with different types of pendulums. Some practitioners prefer crystal pendulums, while others prefer metal or wood. Each type of pendulum has its own unique energy and symbolism, so it is important to find one that resonates with you.

Ultimately, the key to successful pendulum divination is to trust your intuition and let go of any expectations or preconceived notions. Allow the pendulum to guide you and trust that the answers you receive are for your highest good.

With time and practice, you will develop a deep and meaningful relationship with your pendulum, unlocking the mysteries of the universe and gaining invaluable insights into your life and the world around you.

Creating Sacred Space for Pendulum Divination

Before starting your pendulum session, and any peel into the intricacies of this ancient practice, it is essential to understand the importance of creating a sacred space for pendulum divination. The effects of the pendulum's movements can be adversely affected by outside energies, plus the ever present "wish fulfillment" energies. This is where your own hopes of a specific answer will actually cause the pendulum to give false answers.

Because of the sensitivity of the pendulum to outside

energies, it's important to create a sealed energy, sacred space for your work with a pendulum. Use any high magik method of creating a circle. Or simply visualize a circle of golden light surrounding your spot, and envision this golden energy filling the space, pushing out any negative energy.

A sacred space is a designated area where practitioners can connect with the higher realms and channel their energy into the divination process. To create a sacred space for pendulum divination, start by selecting a quiet and undisturbed corner of your living space. This area should be cleansed and purified before each session. Burning frankincense or using cleansing crystals can help remove any negative energies and provide a blank canvas for your magikal workings.

Next, set up an altar or a focal point in your sacred space. This can be a simple arrangement of meaningful objects, such as crystals, candles, or symbols, that resonate with your spiritual journey. The altar serves as a physical representation of your intent and acts as a focal point for your divination practice.

It is crucial to create an atmosphere of tranquility and serenity within your sacred space. Consider incorporating soft lighting and soothing music to enhance the ambiance. It's as if you're going to seduce your pendulum. Just go easy on the flowers.

Lighting candles or incense can also help in creating a meditative environment conducive to divination.

Before commencing your pendulum divination session, it is important to ground and center yourself. Engage in a brief meditation or breathing exercise to calm the mind and connect with your higher self. By doing so, you align your energies with the magikal forces at play and prepare yourself to receive accurate insights from the pendulum.

Remember, the sacred space you create for pendulum divination is not limited to a physical location. It extends beyond the realm of the visible and encompasses the energetic field surrounding you. Therefore, it is essential to maintain and nurture this space by regularly cleansing and recharging its energy.

By creating a sacred space for pendulum divination, you invite the divine guidance and wisdom to flow through you. This allows your pendulum to become a powerful tool for self- discovery, spiritual growth, and unlocking the secrets of the universe.

Asking Yes/No Questions and Interpreting Answers

In divination, the pendulum is a powerful tool for divination, offering insights and guidance from the spiritual realm. As divination students, it is crucial to understand the art of asking yes/no questions and interpreting the answers received through the pendulum. This chapter will take a deep dive into the intricacies of this process, providing you with the knowledge and skills necessary to master pendulum divination.

When asking yes/no questions, it is important to formulate them clearly and concisely.

Ambiguity in your queries may lead to confusing or inaccurate responses. Begin by holding the pendulum in your dominant hand, allowing it to hang freely. Center yourself, focus your intention, and ask your question with determination.

As the pendulum swings, its movements will indicate the answer to your question. A back- and-forth swing usually signifies a "yes" response, while a side-to-side motion indicates a "no" answer. It is essential to establish a baseline by asking a few simple questions whose answers you already know. This will help you understand the pendulum's unique language and ensure accurate interpretations.

Interpreting the answers received through the pendulum requires intuition and a deep connection to your spiritual self. Keep in mind that the pendulum is a conduit between the physical and spiritual realms. Therefore, it is important to trust your instincts and rely on your inner wisdom when deciphering the messages conveyed.

Sometimes, the pendulum may exhibit hesitant or unclear movements, which could indicate a lack of clarity or a question that is not suitable for a yes/no response. In such cases, it is advisable to rephrase your question or seek guidance through alternative divination methods.

Remember, the pendulum is a sacred tool that requires respect and reverence. Treat it as a conduit for divine guidance and approach your divination sessions with a calm and open mind. Regular practice and deepening your connection with the pendulum will enhance your skills and sharpen your interpretations over time.

In conclusion, mastering the art of asking yes/no questions and interpreting answers through the pendulum is an essential skill for students of high magik. By formulating clear questions, establishing a baseline, and trusting your intuition, you can unlock the profound wisdom and guidance offered by this powerful divination tool. Embrace the pendulum as your ally on the path of high magik and let its movements illuminate your journey.

Using Charts and Answer Wheels

In this section, we'll go over the other various methods of obtaining an answer using simple charts. Once you have a sacred space to work in, knowing that the pendulum will not be influenced by outside energies or forces, you will want to move beyond yes/no questions.

In the APPENDIX, you'll find a couple of pendulum answer charts. The best I have found thus far is from a document called "Letter to Robin". That method is an answer wheel, with areas for Yes/No, followed by a wheel with numbers and letters. Then what I call "Half-Circle Charts", where you take the time to figure out the possible answers, then write those into the blank areas, then start your session.

There are also a lot of books with pendulum charts, but I usually make my own, with a half circle divided into even parts. This allows me to easily see which answer the pendulum is giving me. When you have a chart with a full circle, it's sometimes not clear where you should read the answer. A half-circle leaves no room for doubt.

Dowsing: Using the Pendulum to Find Objects or Information

In the realm of high magik, where the powers of divination hold immense significance, the art of dowsing with a pendulum is an essential skill to master. This ancient technique allows us to tap into the hidden energies of the universe to seek answers, locate objects, and access valuable information that may otherwise remain concealed.

The pendulum, a small weight suspended on a string or chain, serves as a powerful tool for divination. It acts as a conduit between our conscious and subconscious minds, enabling us to receive intuitive guidance from the spiritual realm. The pendulum's movements, governed by the energy we emit, can provide us with clear and concise responses to our queries.

To begin your journey into the world of pendulum divination, it is crucial to choose a pendulum that resonates with your energy. This could be a crystal, metal, or wooden pendulum, as long as it feels right for you. Take the time to cleanse and charge your pendulum before use, ensuring that it is attuned to your personal vibrations.

Once you have established a connection with your pendulum, you can start using it to find objects or obtain information. Begin by holding the pendulum between your thumb and forefinger, allowing it to hang freely. Clear your mind and focus on your intention. You may choose to ask specific questions or simply seek guidance on a particular matter.

As you pose your questions, observe the pendulum's movements. It may swing back and forth, move in circles, or remain stationary. Each movement carries a distinct meaning and should be interpreted accordingly. For example, a back-and-forth swing may indicate a positive response, while a circular motion could signify uncertainty or a negative answer.

As with any divination practice, it is crucial to cultivate patience and trust in your intuition. The pendulum acts as a channel for the divine energies, and your subconscious mind holds the key to unlocking its true potential. The more you practice, the stronger your connection will become, and the more accurate your divination readings will be.

Remember, dowsing with a pendulum is not limited to physical objects. It can also be used to access information from the spiritual realm, such as guidance from spirit guides or insight into past lives. With time and dedication, you will become adept at harnessing the power of the pendulum to uncover the hidden truths that shape your magikal journey.

In conclusion, mastering the art of dowsing with a pendulum is an essential skill for any high magik student. By using this ancient divination tool, you can tap into the vast energies of the universe and access valuable information that may otherwise remain elusive. With practice and dedication, you will unlock the true potential of the pendulum and embark on a transformative journey of self-discovery and enlightenment.

Mapping: Utilizing the Pendulum for Spatial Analysis

Remember, the pendulum is a powerful tool that can be harnessed for various purposes, including divination. One such application of the pendulum is in spatial analysis, where it can assist students in mapping out energy fields, ley lines, and other mystical phenomena. This subchapter delves into the intricacies of utilizing the pendulum for spatial analysis, providing high magik students with the knowledge and techniques needed to navigate unseen realms.

My grandfather used to use his pendulum to map out water lines and to find buried wires. He'd need to locate a line in the yard, and I'd watch as he walked back and forth, holding the pendulum. His was a simple wooden ball, suspended by a small chain. Somewhere, my mother still has his old pendulum.

Understanding the significance of mapping in the realm of high magik is crucial. By mapping out energetic patterns and ley lines, students can gain insights into the flow of energy within a specific area. This knowledge is invaluable for practitioners seeking to identify potent energy spots, create sacred spaces, or connect with specific spiritual entities. The pendulum serves as a reliable compass, guiding students through the intricacies of the energetic landscape.

To begin the journey into mapping with a pendulum,

students must first attune themselves to the pendulum's energy. This involves cleansing and charging the pendulum, as well as establishing a clear intention for its use. By forging a strong connection with the pendulum, students can tap into its divinatory abilities and gain accurate insights into the energies they seek to map.

Once attunement is achieved, students can start the process of mapping by physically surveying the area of interest. Whether it is a forest, a cityscape, or a specific building, the pendulum can assist in identifying energy hotspots, ley lines, and other energetic phenomena. By systematically moving through the area and observing the pendulum's responses, students can create a detailed map that highlights the energetic dynamics present.

Moreover, students will learn to interpret the pendulum's movements and vibrations, which provide valuable clues about the nature and intensity of the energies encountered. This allows for a deeper understanding of the energetic landscape and enhances the ability to harness and manipulate these forces for various magikal purposes.

As people progress in their understanding of spatial analysis with the pendulum, they will gain the skills to create comprehensive maps that serve as powerful tools for future magikal endeavors. These maps can be used to plan rituals, enhance spellwork, or unlock hidden knowledge within a given area.

Ultimately, mastering the pendulum for spatial analysis empowers high magik students to explore and manipulate the unseen realms with precision and intention. By unlocking the secrets of the energetic landscape, practitioners can tap into the full potential of their craft and embark on transformative journeys of spiritual discovery.

Energy Detection: Sensing Vibrations and Auras with the Pendulum

Energy detection is where we will now learn to sense vibrations and auras using the powerful tool that is the pendulum. I have mapped someone's chakras using the pendulum, and I have also energized and charged the chakras with it.

As magicians, you understand that everything around us is composed of energy. Every person, object, and even thought emits its unique vibrational frequency. By harnessing the innate powers of the pendulum, we can tap into these energetic vibrations and gain profound insights into the unseen.

To begin, it is essential to attune yourself to the pendulum's energy field. Sit in a calm and focused state, holding your pendulum with a relaxed grip.

Close your eyes and take a few deep breaths,

allowing your mind to quiet and your body to become receptive.

Once you feel centered, gently ask the pendulum to show you the energy vibrations around you. Slowly move the pendulum in a circular motion, allowing it to swing freely. As you do so, visualize your consciousness expanding, reaching out to sense the subtle energy fields surrounding you.

Observe the pendulum's movements carefully. Does it swing in a particular direction or pattern? Pay attention to its speed and intensity. These movements serve as your map, guiding you towards the energies present in your environment.

For example, I have found the crown chakra causes the pendulum to swing in a clockwise manner, then reverse when over the 3rd eye chakra. This back and forth continues as I scan the person.

As you continue to practice, you will develop a heightened sensitivity to energy vibrations.

With time, you will be able to differentiate between various types of energies, whether they emanate from living beings or inanimate objects. You may even detect the residual energy of past events or the ethereal aura of individuals.

Remember, the pendulum is merely a conduit, a tool

that amplifies your intuitive abilities. Your mind and intention are the true drivers of energy detection. Trust your instincts and allow your intuition to guide you in interpreting the pendulum's messages.

Energy detection with the pendulum offers a gateway to a deeper understanding of the interconnectedness of all things. It allows you to navigate the energetic tapestry that surrounds us, unveiling hidden truths and illuminating the path to personal growth and spiritual development.

So, gang, embrace the power of the pendulum and embark on this extraordinary journey of energy detection. Master this art, and you will unlock a world of infinite possibilities, enhancing your magikal practice and expanding your consciousness beyond the mundane.

Developing Your Intuition and Trusting the Pendulum

Exercises and Practices

When it comes to the world of high magik, achieving mastery in the skill of divination is of utmost importance. The pendulum, which is a mystical instrument, has been proven to be one of the most effective tools for unlocking the secrets of the universe. However, the true power of the pendulum lies not just in its physical form but in the intuitive connection it establishes with the practitioner.

To harness the full potential of the pendulum, it is essential for students of high magik to enhance their intuition. This small section will look at various exercises and practices that can help develop and refining this crucial skill.

Meditation and Visualization: Begin your journey by cultivating a calm and focused mind through meditation. Visualize yourself surrounded by a sphere of white light, allowing it to cleanse and purify your energy. Envision a clear channel connecting you to the universal wisdom, enabling a strong intuitive connection.

Pendulum Alignment: Before every divination session, align yourself with the pendulum's energy. Hold it in your dominant hand and allow it to swing freely. Observe its movements and ensure it is in harmony with your energy. This alignment will facilitate a smoother flow of intuition.

Pendulum Calibration: Calibrating your pendulum is vital to establish a common language between you and the pendulum. Begin by asking simple yes or no questions, noting the distinct movements associated with each response. This calibration process will enhance your ability to interpret the pendulum's messages accurately.

Energy Clearing: Regularly cleanse your pendulum by passing it through incense smoke or placing it under moonlight. This ensures any residual energy is released, allowing for a fresh and clear connection. Additionally, visualize a stream of pure white light flowing through the pendulum, further purifying its energy.

Intuition-Building Exercises: Engage in exercises that stimulate and strengthen your intuition. Practice sensing the energy of objects, people, or situations without relying on external cues. Trust your instincts and gradually expand your abilities through consistent practice.

Journaling: Maintain a divination journal to record your pendulum readings and intuitive insights. Reflecting on past experiences will help identify patterns, strengthen your understanding of symbolism, and enhance your overall intuitive abilities.

Remember, enhancing intuition is a continuous process. Dedicate regular time to these exercises and practices, and be patient with yourself as you develop this essential skill. By honing your intuition, you will unlock the true power of the pendulum, delving deeper into the realms of high magik and uncovering the profound wisdom that awaits.

Chapter Four

Introduction to the Tarot

As I've written previously, I got my first tarot deck with I was 22. I had seen them before, given that several of my friends loved the things. It was a fad for a while in this small apartment (party) complex I lived in for a year during my Junior year at the University of Texas. It seemed just about every other young woman had to practice reading for us guys. I had a suspicion some of the girls were using the cards as a way to meet the guys. And it worked.

Later, I'd bought a Tarot deck because a current girlfriend insisted I needed them. I also got that black cover book to go with them. Man, talk about arcane and pessimistic interpretations.

That put me off the cards for several years. Then I'd drag that deck and book out, try again, then get perturbed about the readings.

I eventually found a book that helped me truly unlock the cards and their messages. That took about 10 years, so hopefully you can use this information and skip the searching that I did. I have that book's title in the appendix, along with the ISBN number to assist you in finding it online.

I can only go over the major points of each card's interpretation. To go fully into my way of looking at each card, I'd likely need an entire book on this subject. My personal interpretation of each card is based upon decades of doing Tarot readings, for myself and others. I can drop a few cards onto the table, then I get the meanings quite clearly, as it activates my own psychic powers to see, or feel, the answer.

So, we'll look at the more traditional meanings of the cards, along with some well-known card spreads. I've blended my personal interpretations of the cards where needed, but you must understand, my interpretations are based upon my own use of the cards. After working with the cards for a lengthy period, you will also begin to see what each card means, and what that card means in relation to both the question and the position in the spread. It's also quite important that you record your readings, even the practice readings, so you can see what happens later and connect the cards seen in the reading to what has happened.

Also, please note that I only use the Rider-Wight Tarot deck, so all my descriptions and interpretations are based upon those cards.

Understanding the Tarot

The Tarot deck is a powerful tool that has been used for centuries to unlock the mysteries of the human experience. Tarot card reading and interpretation is just one of the many practices that can be explored using the Tarot deck. It is also a valuable tool for those interested in astrology and horoscope analysis, scrying, and pendulum dowsing. By delving into the complexities of the Tarot deck, people can unlock a world of spiritual insight and personal growth.

With a total of 78 cards, the Tarot deck is divided into two major categories, namely the Major Arcana and the Minor Arcana. The Major Arcana, which comprises 22 cards, is a collection of significant archetypes or universal themes that are represented by each card. Not only do these cards offer profound insights into the human condition and spiritual journey, but they also hold deep symbolic meanings that can be interpreted in a multitude of ways.

Comprising four distinct suits - Wands, Cups, Swords, and Pentacles - the Minor Arcana comprises 56 cards that are an essential part of the Tarot card deck. The four suits in the deck of cards represent the four distinct elements that are fire, water, air, and earth; and each of these elements corresponds to a variety of aspects in life, including creativity, emotions, intellect, and material abundance. It is of utmost importance to have a clear comprehension of the suits and their corresponding significances in order to make precise interpretations. Please note, the "regular" playing cards were developed from the Tarot, with clubs = wands, hearts = cups, coins = diamonds, and spades = swords.

The Tarot deck is rich in symbolism. Each card is adorned with intricate illustrations and intricate details that convey hidden messages and esoteric knowledge. As a high magic student, it is crucial to explore the symbolic language of the Tarot, as it provides a gateway to profound insights and intuitive revelations.

To unlock the power of the Tarot deck, one must develop a deep connection with the cards. This can be achieved through regular practice and meditation. By handling the cards frequently and studying their imagery, you will begin to attune yourself to their energies and develop your intuition.

When getting a new tarot deck, I recommend spending a lot of time shuffling the new deck, but only after a general cleaning. The best way to cleanse a new deck is by placing it into a plastic bag filled with regular salt. Salt is salt, and after decades of using salts to cleanse an object, I have found no difference between table salt and expensive sea salt. I always have a box of pickling salt in the pantry for this purpose (plus cooking, of course). (And pickling... but I don't do a lot of pickling, so it's for cooking and cleansing stuff.)

Apart from familiarizing yourself with the significance of every card, it is also necessary to master at least a couple of Tarot spreads, a method of narrating a story with the help of Tarot, and simultaneously getting a glimpse of the energy that encircles the question. Learning various Tarot spreads is essential for effective divination. Spreads determine the layout and arrangement of the cards and offer different perspectives on a particular issue or question. The experimentation of different spreads is a beneficial practice for you to find the ones that resonate with you the most.

Lastly, ethical considerations are paramount when practicing Tarot card reading and interpretation. As a magik student, it is crucial to approach the Tarot with respect, integrity, and a genuine desire to help others. Honoring the sacredness of the practice and ensuring the privacy and well-being of those seeking guidance is of utmost importance. Therefore, I rarely do a reading on someone for someone else. It just isn't ethical, and you can also receive bad information, because the target's higher self and guides may choose to block or mislead you.

Another thing to note - my work with the Tarot has shown me the futility of trying to fathom meaning out of reversed cards. As a result, about thirty years ago, I stopped worrying about reversed cards, and my readings are still quite accurate.

Remember, the Tarot is not merely a tool, but a gateway to ancient wisdom and profound insights into the mysteries of the universe.

Chapter Five

The Tarot: The Major Arcana

The Tarot is divided into two parts. One, the Major Arcana, also known as "Trump" cards, and they're a special group of cards known. These cards hold the key to unlocking the deepest secrets of the universe and offer profound insights into the human condition. The other part is the Minor Arcana, which we'll look at in the next section.

The Major Arcana consists of 22 cards, each representing a different archetype or spiritual concept. These cards possess an undeniable magnetism, drawing tarot card reading and interpretation enthusiasts, astrology and horoscope analysts, and practitioners of various divination techniques like scrying and pendulum dowsing into their mystical embrace.

As a practitioner of high magic, it is crucial to understand the significance of the Major Arcana and its role in divination practices. These cards are not just pieces of beautifully illustrated paper; they are gateways to higher consciousness and portals to hidden realms. Each card carries its own unique symbolism, requiring a deep understanding and intuitive connection to unravel their profound messages.

From the Fool, symbolizing new beginnings and infinite possibilities, to the World, representing completion and wholeness, the Major Arcana takes us on a transformative journey through life's trials and triumphs. Each card reveals important life lessons and spiritual growth opportunities, urging us to explore our inner selves and embrace the wisdom of the universe.

Astrology enthusiasts will find correlations between the Major Arcana and the celestial bodies. The Fool, for instance, embodies the energy of Uranus, representing sudden and unexpected change. The High Priestess resonates with the lunar energy, representing intuition and hidden knowledge. By delving into these connections, astrology and horoscope analysts can enhance their interpretations and offer a more comprehensive understanding of the cosmos.

For practitioners of divination techniques like

scrying and pendulum dowsing, the Major Arcana can serve as powerful focal points.

In conclusion, the Major Arcana is a captivating and essential part of the Tarot deck. Its profound symbolism, spiritual concepts, and connections to astrology and divination techniques make it a treasure trove of wisdom for high magic students. By delving into the mysteries of the Major Arcana, practitioners can unlock the secrets of the universe and gain invaluable insights into their own lives and the world around them.

Exploring the Fool's Journey

I'm calling this sub-chapter "Exploring the Fool's Journey" in this book. Here, we will delve into one of the most intriguing and profound aspects of interpreting Tarot cards – the Fool's Journey.

The Fool's Journey is a concept that lies at the very heart of Tarot symbolism, representing a transformative and enlightening path that the Fool embarks upon as they journey through the 22 Major Arcana cards. This journey mirrors our own personal and spiritual growth, offering us guidance and insight into our lives.

As we begin to interpret Tarot cards, it is vital to understand the symbolism and significance of the Fool's Journey. The Fool, often depicted as a carefree traveler, represents the seeker within each of us who is open to new experiences and possibilities. The Fool sets out on their adventure, encountering various archetypal figures and life lessons along the way.

Each Major Arcana card encountered by the Fool represents a distinct stage in their spiritual evolution. From the Empress representing nurturing and abundance, to the Death card symbolizing transformation and rebirth, every card carries its own unique message and wisdom. By exploring the Fool's Journey, we gain a deeper understanding of the Tarot's profound teachings.

Interpreting Tarot cards through the Fool's Journey allows us to connect with our own life experiences and challenges. By recognizing the parallels between the Fool's path and our own personal journey, we can gain clarity, guidance, and spiritual growth. The Fool's Journey invites us to embrace life's uncertainties, learn from our mistakes, and celebrate our victories.

Moreover, the Fool's Journey is not a linear progression, but rather a cyclical process. As we continue interpreting Tarot cards, we understand that the Fool's Journey is not a onetime experience but a recurring cycle of growth and self-discovery. This cyclical nature reminds us that life is a continuous journey of learning and evolving.

Ready? So, off we go!

The Fool

Embrace the Journey of Infinite Possibilities

In the Tarot, The Fool is undoubtedly one of the most enigmatic and captivating cards. Representing the beginning of the Major Arcana's journey, The Fool signifies a fresh start, unlimited potential, and a leap of faith into the unknown. Let's take a look at the profound symbolism and interpretations behind The Fool, providing valuable insights for people interpreting Tarot cards.

As you gaze upon The Fool, you are instantly captivated by the figure's carefree demeanor, oblivious to the precipice before them. This card serves as a reminder that embarking on any new venture requires courage and a willingness to let go of fear. The Fool encourages students of high magik to embrace the unknown, for it is only through taking risks that one can truly grow and progress on their spiritual path.

The Fool represents innocence, spontaneity, and a childlike curiosity. It signifies a time of new beginnings and limitless potential. When The Fool appears in a reading, it suggests that the querent is at the cusp of a transformative journey, urging them to trust their instincts and follow their heart's calling.

However, The Fool also serves as a cautionary tale. Its depiction of a naïve figure on the edge of a precipice reminds students of high magik that blind faith can lead to recklessness. The Fool teaches the importance of balance, urging the querent to embrace their sense of adventure while also considering the consequences of their actions.

Furthermore, The Fool is associated with the element of Air, symbolizing intellect, intuition, and communication. It encourages students of high magik to embrace their intellectual curiosity and explore new ideas and perspectives. The Fool reminds us that we are forever students, continuously evolving and expanding our knowledge.

In conclusion, The Fool is a powerful archetype that beckons students of high magik and enthusiasts of interpreting Tarot cards to embark on a journey of self-discovery and growth. Through The Fool, we learn to trust our instincts, embrace new beginnings, and welcome the unknown. By understanding the symbolism and interpretations behind The Fool, we unlock the mysteries of the Tarot and gain valuable insights into our own spiritual paths. May The Fool guide you on your quest for wisdom, enlightenment, and infinite possibilities.

The Magician

Now, we come to The Magician, a powerful archetype that embodies the essence of manifestation and manipulation.

The Magician, represented by card number one in the Tarot deck, holds a prominent position as the bridge between the spiritual and physical realms. This card serves as a reminder that we possess the ability to shape our reality through our thoughts, actions, and intentions. It is a symbol of unlimited potential and the harnessing of personal power.

When The Magician appears in a reading, it indicates that you have all the tools necessary to manifest your desires. It signifies the presence of creativity, resourcefulness, and confidence within you. This card urges you to tap into your inner magician and use your skills wisely. Whether you seek love, success, or personal growth, The Magician empowers you to take charge of your destiny.

In interpretation, pay attention to the elements present in The Magician's card. The four suits of the Tarot - Wands, Cups, Swords, and Pentacles - symbolize the four elements: fire, water, air, and earth. The Magician's mastery over these elements represents the harmonious balance required for successful manifestation. Understanding how these elements interact will deepen your interpretation and guide you on your spiritual journey.

Furthermore, The Magician reminds us that our thoughts and intentions shape our reality. It encourages you to align your conscious and subconscious minds, ensuring that your thoughts and desires are in harmony. By doing so, you can unlock your true potential and manifest your dreams with ease.

To fully embrace The Magician's energy, practice visualization, affirmations, and meditation. Use your knowledge of the Tarot to create powerful spreads that align with your intentions. Remember, a magician is only as strong as their focus and belief in their abilities.

I used to see this card pop up in readings I'd do for myself. I finally came to understand this was representing my own self and my own journey as a magician and psychic. When I faced this fact, the card stopped appearing in readings unless I chose it as my significator card. (More on these in the Spread chapter of the Tarot section.)

The High Priestess

The High Priestess is a card of profound wisdom and hidden knowledge, offering a gateway to deeper spiritual insights. In tarot card interpretation, The High Priestess holds a significant place, symbolizing the mystery and intuition that lies within us all. As students of high magik and enthusiasts of interpreting tarot cards, understanding the profound messages conveyed by The High Priestess is crucial to unlocking the mysteries that surround us.

When this card appears in a reading, it signifies a call to tap into our intuition and explore the depths of our subconscious. The High Priestess urges us to trust our instincts and look beyond the surface to gain a deeper understanding of the situations we face. By embracing our intuition, we can access a wellspring of ancient knowledge, enabling us to navigate life's challenges with clarity and grace.

The High Priestess is often depicted as a guardian of ancient secrets, standing between the realms of the conscious and the unconscious. She serves as a reminder that there is more to our existence than what meets the eye. By delving into the realms of the unknown, we can uncover hidden truths and gain insight into our own spiritual journey.

In the context of interpreting tarot cards, The High Priestess encourages us to explore the symbolism and imagery within the deck. Each card holds a wealth of occult wisdom, and by delving into their meaning, we can unlock profound insights into our lives and the world. The High Priestess teaches us to look beyond the literal interpretations and tap into the intuitive connections that exist between the cards.

By understanding The High Priestess' significance

and connecting with her energy, we can unlock the mysteries of the tarot and harness its transformative power. The High Priestess invites us to embark on a quest for knowledge, encouraging us to trust in our intuition and explore the depths of our spiritual selves.

In my readings, depending on the question, I'll also figure this may represent a specific woman with these traits. It all depends on the question, who's asking, and where this card appears in a spread.

The Empress

Now comes The Empress, a card that embodies the divine feminine and the creative power within us all.

When The Empress graces your tarot reading, she represents abundance, nurturing, and fertility. She is a symbol of creation and the nurturing force that brings forth life. Her serene presence encourages you to embrace your own creative abilities and explore the depths of your imagination.

In the tarot deck, The Empress is often depicted as a regal figure seated on a throne adorned with lush greenery. This imagery represents the Earth Mother, reminding us of our connection to nature and the importance of nurturing ourselves and those around us.

As you interpret The Empress card, consider the

areas of your life where you can tap into your creative energy. Are you neglecting your passions and talents? The Empress urges you to reconnect with your creative side and allow it to flourish. Whether it be through art, writing, gardening, or any other form of self- expression, The Empress guides you to embrace your unique gifts and bring forth beauty into the world.

In matters of relationships, The Empress signifies love, compassion, and fertility. If you are seeking a romantic connection, this card suggests that love is on the horizon. It may also indicate the possibility of pregnancy or the nurturing of a new relationship.

Remember, The Empress encourages us to nurture ourselves and others, fostering a deep connection based on love and understanding.

When The Empress appears in a career or financial reading, it signifies abundance and success. This card encourages you to trust in your intuition and embrace your creativity in the workplace. It may also indicate a period of financial stability and material comfort.

As you explore the depths of tarot interpretation, allow The Empress to guide you on a journey of self-discovery and creative expression. Embrace her energy, tap into your inner creativity, and unlock the mysteries of your own divine feminine power.

The Emperor

Harness the Power of Authority and Structure

Now here's The Emperor card, a symbol of authority, structure, and unwavering power in the realm of tarot.

When The Emperor appears in a tarot reading, it signifies a strong and influential figure in your life. This could represent a person, an institution, or even an aspect of yourself that embodies the qualities of leadership and control. As you interpret this card, it is vital to consider the context of the reading and the surrounding cards to grasp the full meaning it holds.

The Emperor serves as a reminder of the importance of structure and organization in our lives. It calls upon us to establish a solid foundation, much like an emperor would build a kingdom. This card urges us to take control, make decisions, and establish boundaries. It suggests that by embracing discipline and structure, we can bring order to chaos and achieve great things.

In matters of career or business, The Emperor signifies a time of stability and success. It encourages you to tap into your own leadership potential and be assertive in your professional endeavors. This card indicates that you have the capacity to build a solid career and make long-lasting achievements. However, it also reminds you to balance your assertiveness with compassion and empathy to maintain harmonious relationships with colleagues and employees.

On a personal level, The Emperor highlights the need for self-discipline and personal responsibility. It encourages you to take charge of your life, set goals, and work diligently towards them. This card advises you to keep your emotions in check and approach situations with a calm and rational mindset. By embodying the qualities of The Emperor, you can navigate the complexities of life with confidence and authority.

As you explore the depths of tarot and delve into the mysteries it holds, remember that The Emperor is not about wielding power over others, but rather about finding balance and structure within yourself. Embrace the qualities of authority, discipline, and responsibility, and you will discover a newfound sense of control and empowerment in your spiritual journey.

The Emperor awaits your embrace, ready to guide you on a path of self-discovery and personal growth.

The Hierophant

Unveiling the Secrets of Divine Wisdom

Next up is The Hierophant, unlocking the mysteries surrounding this powerful archetype, revealing its profound symbolism and guiding principles.

The Hierophant card epitomizes the connection between the earthly and divine realms, acting as a conduit for sacred knowledge and spiritual wisdom. As you embark on your journey of interpreting tarot cards, understanding the essence of The Hierophant will provide you with deep insights and guidance.

At first glance, The Hierophant portrays a wise figure seated on a throne, adorned in ceremonial vestments, and holding a symbol of divine authority. This card symbolizes tradition, religious beliefs, and the pursuit of higher knowledge. It urges us to seek guidance from established institutions and ancient wisdom, encouraging us to find strength in a higher power.

In interpreting The Hierophant, we must explore its multifaceted meanings. On one level, it represents a desire for conformity and adherence to societal norms. It encourages us to embrace structure, tradition, and established rules. However, it also reminds us of the importance of questioning authority and seeking personal truth within these frameworks.

The Hierophant calls upon us to embrace our inner spiritual teacher, to seek enlightenment through introspection and introspection. It invites us to find our own path, blending the wisdom of tradition with our unique experiences and perspectives. It reminds us that true understanding comes from a harmonious balance between external guidance and personal intuition.

As students of high magik, you possess a profound ability to read beyond the surface- level symbolism of The Hierophant. Dive deep into the card's imagery, colors, and accompanying symbols to unravel its hidden messages. Pay attention to the keys it presents, revealing the secrets of divine wisdom and the power of spiritual connection.

Remember, The Hierophant serves as a reminder to honor our spiritual journey, seeking knowledge and wisdom from both ancient traditions and our inner selves. As you interpret this card, embrace the transformative power it holds, allowing it to guide you on your path to unlocking the mysteries of tarot and high magik.

Key take-away: The Hierophant illuminates your quest for spiritual enlightenment, empowering you to become a master of interpreting tarot cards and a conduit of divine knowledge.

The Lovers

A Profound Journey of Union and Choice

Sometimes, this card doesn't mean what it might say on the surface. In a reading, it might not really indicate someone will be a lover or partner, and you will have to dig deeper for the correct meaning.

The Lovers card, with its enchanting imagery and intricate symbolism, holds the key to unlocking the mysteries of love, relationships, and choices. The Lovers card goes beyond surface-level interpretations and takes us on a spiritual quest.

At first glance, The Lovers card depicts a man and a woman, standing beneath a heavenly figure, often symbolizing an angel or divine presence. This card represents not only the merging of two souls but also the eternal dance between the conscious and the unconscious, the physical and the spiritual. It teaches us that true love transcends the material realm and reaches into the depths of our souls.

In the realm of relationships, The Lovers card signifies harmony, connection, and the power of choice. It reminds us that love is not just an emotion but a conscious decision we make each day. Through the Lovers card, we are encouraged to explore the depths of our relationships, to nurture and cherish the connections that bring us joy and growth.

However, The Lovers card also challenges us to make choices. It serves as a reminder that the path of love is not always straightforward, and we may encounter crossroads where decisions must be made. These choices may not solely revolve around romantic relationships but may extend to other areas of our lives as well – career, friendships, and personal growth. The Lovers card encourages us to listen to our hearts, trust our intuition, and make choices aligned with our deepest values.

As students of any magik, you are equipped with the knowledge and wisdom to interpret the Tarot cards, but The Lovers card reminds us that this journey is not solely intellectual. It calls upon us to embrace our intuition, connect with our higher selves, and channel the energy of love and union into our readings.

Through The Lovers card, we learn that love is the greatest force in the universe – it unites, heals, and guides us on our spiritual paths. So, as we continue our exploration of interpreting Tarot cards, let us remember the profound teachings of The Lovers card and embark on a journey of love, connection, and conscious choices.

The Chariot

When The Chariot appears in a Tarot reading, it

signifies triumph, willpower, and determination. It represents the ability to overcome obstacles and achieve victory through sheer force of character. The charioteer is depicted as a warrior, representing our inner strength and the control we have over our lives. This card urges us to harness our personal power and take charge of our destiny.

It can also represent, in the reading's context and placement in a spread, the need for speed, or the speed of an event coming at the querent. This card usually, always, appears when something is coming at me, to help me prepare for the event or person it represents.

For students of high magic, The Chariot holds even deeper significance. It represents the charioteer's mastery over the four elements: earth, air, fire, and water. Each of these elements corresponds to different aspects of our lives and magical practices. The earth element signifies practicality and grounding, while air represents intellect and communication. Fire symbolizes passion and transformation, while water embodies emotions and intuition.

When interpreting The Chariot in a high magic context, it is essential to consider how these elements align with our current situation. Are we utilizing our intellect and communication skills effectively? Are we grounded and practical in our magical practices? Are we harnessing the power of passion and transformation to create positive change? Are we in tune with our emotions and intuition?

Furthermore, The Chariot also symbolizes the union of opposites and the balancing of dualities. The black and white sphinxes represent the opposing forces within us, such as light and dark, masculine and feminine, or conscious and unconscious. The charioteer's ability to control and harmonize these opposing forces demonstrates a mastery of balance and integration.

In high magic, the interpretation of The Chariot prompts students to explore the balance between different aspects of their magical practices. It encourages them to embrace both the light and dark aspects of their craft and find harmony within themselves.

In conclusion, The Chariot represents triumph, willpower, and determination, while also symbolizing the mastery of the four elements and the balance of opposing forces. By understanding and embracing the deeper meanings of The Chariot, students of high magic can unlock new insights and enhance their magical practices.

Strength

The Strength card holds a special place. It is a card that transcends the boundaries of the physical world and delves deep into the inner strength of the human spirit. The key to a reading lies in understanding the nuances of this card and harnessing its transformative power.

At first glance, the Strength card may seem straightforward, depicting a figure gently taming a ferocious lion. However, its true significance lies in its symbolism and the lessons it imparts. This card represents the control and mastery of one's primal instincts and emotions, showcasing the tremendous power that lies within each of us.

Interpreting the Strength card requires a deep introspection into one's own fears, desires, and vulnerabilities. It urges us to confront our inner demons and find the courage to overcome them. It reminds us that true strength comes from within, not through external displays of force or dominance.

By featuring self-discipline and self-control, the Strength card reminds us of how essential these traits are in life. One of the key benefits of practicing this is that it helps to cultivate inner fortitude, which ultimately empowers the practitioner to overcome any challenges or obstacles that may arise on their spiritual path. If an individual uses the energy that is represented in this card, they have the ability to access their internal resources and overcome any obstacle or difficulty.

The Strength card also highlights the transformative power of love and compassion. It teaches us that true strength lies in the ability to show kindness and empathy, even in the face of adversity. By embodying this compassionate strength, we can not only tame our own inner beasts, but also inspire and uplift those around us.

It's crucial to remember that the Strength card is not merely about physical strength or dominance. It transcends the limitations of the material world and urges us to tap into our spiritual essence. It reminds us that true power lies in the connection between mind, body, and spirit.

In conclusion, the Strength card encourages self-reflection, inner strength, and the transformative power of love and compassion. By embracing these teachings, practitioners can unlock their true potential and embark on a journey of spiritual growth and self-discovery.

The Hermit

Delving into the Depths of Solitude

Now, we'll explore the enigmatic archetype of The Hermit and unlock the secrets hidden within its symbolism. As we delve into the depths of solitude, we will discover the profound wisdom and transformative power that awaits those who seek the guidance of this card.

The Hermit represents a profound spiritual journey. This card invites us to embrace solitude, introspection, and self-discovery. It serves as a gentle reminder that sometimes, the answers we seek lie within ourselves, waiting to be uncovered through inner reflection.

The Hermit is often depicted as an old sage, cloaked in darkness, holding a lantern aloft to illuminate the path ahead. This lantern symbolizes the light of knowledge and wisdom, guiding us through the shadows of uncertainty. It reminds us that by embracing solitude and withdrawing from the distractions of the external world, we can uncover profound insights and gain a deeper understanding of ourselves and the universe.

This section will investigate the various interpretations of The Hermit, this card can represent a period of introspection, spiritual enlightenment, and the search for inner truth. Ponder the practical applications of The Hermit's energy in our daily lives, such as the need for self-care, seeking solitude to recharge, and the importance of meditation and mindfulness practices.

As students, it is essential to approach The Hermit with an open mind and a willingness to explore the depths of our own being. Remember, this is a transformative journey, shedding light on the mysteries of solitude and self-discovery. So, let us embrace the wisdom of The Hermit and unlock the transformative power it holds within its ancient symbology.

The Wheel of Fortune

Embracing the Cycles of Life

The Wheel of Fortune card is a powerful symbol of destiny, karma, and the ever- changing nature of existence. It represents the perpetual motion of life's cycles, reminding us that nothing remains constant and that change is the only constant. As you study magik and the Tarot, you begin to understand that the universe operates in a cyclical pattern, and this card reflects that truth.

When interpreting The Wheel of Fortune in a tarot reading, it signifies the ebb and flow of fortune, both good and bad. This card reminds us that life is a series of ups and downs, and we must learn to navigate its ever-changing landscape. It teaches us to embrace the highs and lows, understanding that each experience serves a purpose in our personal and spiritual growth.

The Wheel of Fortune also represents the concept of destiny and the influence of karma. It reminds us that our actions have consequences and that we are responsible for shaping our own fate. By interpreting this card, we can gain insights into the karmic lessons we are currently facing and the opportunities for growth that lie ahead.

Furthermore, this card encourages us to embrace the

concept of surrender. It advises us to release control over external circumstances and trust in the universal flow. By surrendering to the Wheel of Fortune, we align ourselves with the natural rhythms of the universe, allowing for greater harmony and synchronicity in our lives.

In one book, I had mentioned how the Wheel of Fortune, depending on position in the readings, indicates a time to gamble. Folks, students, gentle readers, let me further add that this isn't a guarantee of winning. However, you possess the unique ability to tap into the energies represented by The Wheel of Fortune.

Through meditation, ritual, and deep introspection, you can unlock the wisdom hidden within this card and apply it to your personal journey.

Justice

Justice is a powerful and profound card in the Tarot deck, holding great significance for those who seek to interpret its message. As students of high magik and practitioners of interpreting Tarot cards, it is crucial to understand the deeper meanings and symbolism behind the Justice card.

In the realm of Tarot, Justice represents balance, fairness, and the consequences of our actions. It embodies the universal principle of cause and effect, reminding us that every action we take has repercussions. This card serves as a reminder that justice will prevail, and that our deeds will ultimately be judged.

When Justice appears in a reading, it urges us to seek equilibrium in our lives. It encourages us to examine our choices, decisions, and behaviors, ensuring that we are treating others fairly and acting with integrity. This card reminds us that fairness and honesty are essential in maintaining harmonious relationships and fostering personal growth.

In its imagery, the Justice card often depicts a figure holding a sword and scales. The sword represents truth and discernment, cutting through illusions and revealing the reality of a situation. The scales symbolize the need for balance and impartiality when making judgments. This imagery serves as a gentle reminder to approach situations with clarity and objectivity.

Furthermore, Justice signifies the need to take responsibility for our actions. It prompts us to acknowledge any wrongdoings or mistakes we may have made and seek to make amends. By doing so, we can restore balance and create a more just and equitable future.

In a broader sense, Justice also reminds us of the connectedness of all things. It reflects the interplay between karma and destiny, suggesting that our actions in the present can shape our future experiences. By understanding this interconnectedness, we can make conscious choices that align with our highest good and the greater good of all.

As students of high magik, the Justice card challenges us to cultivate a sense of fairness and righteousness in our practices. It encourages us to harness our intuitive abilities and divine wisdom to make just decisions and offer guidance to those who seek our counsel. By integrating the lessons of Justice into our journey of interpreting Tarot cards, we can navigate the mysterious realms with integrity, compassion, and wisdom.

Remember, Justice is not merely an external force but also an internal compass that guides us towards living a life of authenticity and truth. Embrace the teachings of this powerful card, and may your interpretations be infused with justice, fairness, and profound insight.

The Hanged Man

The Enigmatic Symbol of Surrender and Transformation

In Tarot cards, one of the most enigmatic and thought-provoking symbols is that of The Hanged Man. As students of high magik and enthusiasts of interpreting Tarot cards, we delve into the depths of this card's meaning, unlocking the mysteries it holds and unraveling its profound significance.

The Hanged Man, depicted as an individual suspended upside down by one leg, challenges our conventional perception of reality and invites us to embrace a new perspective. It symbolizes the act of surrendering, willingly letting go of control, and allowing life to unfold naturally. This card speaks to the transformative power of surrender, urging us to detach ourselves from the ego's desires and expectations.

In Tarot, The Hanged Man often indicates a period of suspended action or a necessary pause in our journey. It suggests that by relinquishing our preconceived notions and embracing a state of surrender; we open ourselves to new insights, wisdom, and personal growth. The Hanged Man teaches us that sometimes, the greatest achievements come not from pushing forward but from surrendering to the flow of life.

The card's imagery also carries a spiritual connotation, reflecting a profound connection to higher realms. The Hanged Man represents a willingness to sacrifice personal desires for the greater good, showing us that enlightenment and spiritual growth often require sacrifices and letting go of worldly attachments.

Interpreting The Hanged Man requires a delicate balance of intuition and introspection. When this card appears in a reading, it may suggest that the querent is at a crossroads, needing to make a difficult decision or embrace a new perspective. It encourages us to reflect on our current circumstances, to pause and assess our priorities, and to trust that the universe has a greater plan in store for us.

We are called to explore the depths of The Hanged Man's symbolism. Through its lessons of surrender, sacrifice, and spiritual growth, this card guides us on a profound journey of self-discovery and transformation. By embracing the wisdom of The Hanged Man, we unlock the mysteries hidden within ourselves and open doors to new realms of possibilities.

Personally, this card often turns up when I'm about to experience a period of no forward movement, I'm literally hung upside down, just waiting. During these periods, I'll often find myself in that position while in bed, trying to sleep. Then I'll meditate to see what is needed to break the stalemate, and to finally move forward.

Death

Embracing Transformation and Renewal

Fear not! Death, within the Tarot deck, does not represent literal death but rather symbolizes the concept of change, transformation, and the inevitability of cycles. It stands as a reminder that in order to grow, we must let go of the old and make space for the new. It signifies the end of one phase and the beginning of another, urging us to embrace the process of shedding our old skin and allowing ourselves to be reborn.

Think of it like a shedding skin on a reptile.

When encountering the Death card during a Tarot reading, it is crucial for you to approach it with an open mind and a willingness to explore the depths of their own psyche. Rather than fearing the unknown, we are encouraged to view this card as an invitation to release attachments, beliefs, and patterns that no longer serve us.

In the journey of life, death is an integral part of the natural cycle. Just as the leaves fall from the trees in autumn, making way for new growth in spring, so too must we let go of what is no longer aligned with our higher purpose. The Death card teaches us that the path to enlightenment and self-realization often involves confronting our fears, dismantling old structures, and surrendering to the transformative power of the universe.

By embracing the Death card, people can tap into their innate potential for growth and evolution. It encourages us to trust in the process of life and death, knowing that every ending is merely a new beginning. Through this understanding, we can navigate the challenges and uncertainties of existence with grace, resilience, and a deep sense of purpose.

As we move further into the mysteries of Tarot, let us remember that the Death card is not an omen of doom, but rather a catalyst for personal and spiritual unfoldment. It serves as a beacon, reminding us to let go of stagnant energies, limiting beliefs, and outdated patterns, paving the way for profound transformation and renewal. Embrace the Death card, and witness the magic that unfolds when we surrender to the cycles of life.

Temperance

The Alchemical Balance Within Tarot Interpretation

Often overlooked, one cannot underestimate the significance of Temperance. This powerful card, often represented by a figure delicately pouring water between two cups, serves as a symbol of balance and moderation. Folks, mastering the art of interpreting tarot cards requires a deep understanding of Temperance and its profound implications.

Temperance teaches us that life is a delicate dance of harmonizing opposing forces. Just as the alchemists sought to transmute base metals into gold, so, too, must we strive to find equilibrium within ourselves and our interpretations.

This card reminds us to temper our emotions, thoughts, and actions in order to achieve a state of divine balance.

When interpreting tarot cards, Temperance calls upon us to blend intuition with reason. It reminds us that the tarot is not a tool for hasty judgment or impulsive decisions, but rather a guide for thoughtful reflection and introspection. By embracing the principles of Temperance, students of high magik can unlock the true mysteries hidden within the cards.

In a reading, the presence of Temperance suggests the need for moderation and patience. It urges us to find the middle ground, avoiding extremes and embracing a more measured approach. This card serves as a gentle reminder that life's challenges can be overcome through the application of tranquility and self-restraint.

Furthermore, Temperance encourages us to seek harmony in our relationships and interactions. It reminds us to listen attentively, communicate honestly, and cultivate empathy. By fostering balance and understanding, we can forge deeper connections with others and create an environment of mutual growth and support.

I feel it is essential to recognize that Temperance extends beyond the confines of tarot interpretation. Its lessons can be applied to all aspects of our lives, guiding us towards spiritual enlightenment and personal growth. By embracing the principles of Temperance, we align ourselves with the universal flow of energy and unlock our true potential.

Interesting to note, this card used to come up a LOT when I was younger, and spending a lot of time with friends, overeating and over drinking. It took me a while, but I finally broke that habit.

The Devil

First off, the "devil" as depicted in this card isn't really a devil, but a daemon. But, since the Tarot uses archetypes, I have to cast off my knowledge of who is, and isn't, "The Devil" and look at this card as it fits into the rest of the Major Arcana.

Few cards evoke as much intrigue and fascination as The Devil. This powerful card symbolizes the darker aspects of our nature, and its presence in a reading often raises eyebrows and piques curiosity. As get into the secrets of interpreting tarot cards, it is vital to understand the significance and potential messages that The Devil carries.

Contrary to popular belief, The Devil card is not an embodiment of pure evil. Instead, it represents the shadow side of humanity, the aspects of ourselves that we often suppress or deny. It symbolizes our desires, addictions, and obsessions – the chains that bind us and prevent personal growth. When this card appears in a reading, it serves as a reminder to confront and acknowledge the darker elements within us.

Interpreting The Devil card requires a delicate balance between caution and understanding. It urges us to examine our attachments and dependencies, whether they are material possessions, relationships, or unhealthy habits. This card encourages us to question if these attachments are truly serving our highest good or if they are hindering our spiritual progress.

The Devil card also highlights the importance of breaking free from the chains that bind us. It is a call to liberation and self-awareness. By confronting and understanding our own personal demons, we can transform our lives and embark on a journey of self-discovery and spiritual growth.

However, it is crucial to approach The Devil card with caution. Its appearance in a reading does not imply that one is doomed or destined for a life of darkness. Rather, it is a gentle reminder to remain vigilant and avoid falling into destructive patterns. The Devil card serves as a guide, urging us to confront our fears and weaknesses, and to take ownership of our actions.

We must remember that The Devil card is not to be feared, but rather embraced as an opportunity for self-reflection and growth. By understanding its symbolism and messages, we can unlock the mysteries it holds and harness its power to transform our lives.

In conclusion, the Devil card calls for self-awareness, liberation, and breaking free from unhealthy attachments. As students of high magik and interpreters of tarot cards, we must approach The Devil card with caution, understanding its profound symbolism and using it as a catalyst for personal transformation. By unlocking the mysteries of The Devil, we unlock the mysteries within ourselves.

I have found it to be very accurate - especially when I was fully into my career as a photographer, and I'd be using models who were slaves to alcohol or drugs. When I'd do a reading for a model, this card would often show up, to say "Hey, stop partying so much, and sober up a bit."

This card appeared in a reading I did for a neighbor and friend. It was paired with Temperance and then the ten of swords (more on that card later). I told him to back off on the drinking, but within two months, he was dead. He was drinking a liter or more of whiskey a day, and eventually, it killed him. Take the warnings seriously when warned by the Tarot!

The Tower

The Tower. Okay, there are few cards I loathe, and this is one, because it's usually quite accurate. I'll see that, and I'll think "Well, better buckle up!" My experience has shown this occurs when one's life is about to get shaken up. The Tower card is a potent and transformative symbol that often strikes fear in the hearts of those unfamiliar with its true essence, for good reason.

Depicting a tall tower engulfed in flames, with a bolt of lightning striking its crown, this card represents sudden and unavoidable change. It is a reminder that sometimes, in order to build something stronger, we must first let go of what no longer serves us.

When interpreting the Tower card, it is crucial to recognize its dual nature. On one hand, it signifies destruction, chaos, and the dismantling of existing structures. This destruction can occur in various aspects of our lives, be it relationships, beliefs, or even our own self-identity. However, it's important to remember that destruction is not always negative. It serves as a catalyst for growth and transformation, clearing the path for new beginnings.

The Tower card also symbolizes divine intervention and the awakening of consciousness. The lightning bolt represents a sudden burst of insight or revelation, shattering illusions and bringing truth to light. It is through this process of destruction and revelation that we can rebuild our lives on a stronger foundation, free from the constraints of the past.

In a Tarot reading, the appearance of the Tower card may indicate that significant upheaval is imminent. It serves as a warning to prepare for change and to be open to embracing new possibilities. While the initial impact may be unsettling, it is essential to trust the process and have faith in the transformative power of the Tower.

It is crucial to remember that the Tower card often does not represent an external force acting upon us, but rather an internal process of growth and evolution. By embracing the lessons of the Tower, we can harness its energy to transcend limitations and create a more authentic and aligned existence.

We must approach this archetype with an open mind and an understanding that change is necessary for growth. Embrace the lightning strikes of the Tower and allow its transformative energy to guide you on your mystical journey of interpreting Tarot cards.

The Star

The Star is a card that holds immense power and significance in the world of Tarot. It is a symbol of hope, inspiration, and divine guidance. While interpreting Tarot cards, The Star serves as a beacon of light, guiding the querent towards a deeper understanding of their spiritual journey.

When The Star appears in a Tarot reading, it signifies a time of renewal and transformation. It represents a period of healing, where old wounds can be mended, and new beginnings can take root. This card reminds us that even in the darkest of times, there is always a glimmer of hope shining through.

The Star is often depicted as a woman pouring water from two jugs, one into a pool and the other onto the land. This symbolism suggests a balance between the emotional and the practical aspects of our lives. It encourages us to find harmony between our dreams and aspirations and the actions we take to manifest them.

In the context of interpreting Tarot cards, The Star encourages students of high magik to embrace their intuition and trust in their inner wisdom. It urges them to have faith in their abilities and to follow their unique path, even when faced with doubt or uncertainty. The Star reminds us that we are all connected to a higher power and that our dreams and desires are not only valid but also essential to our spiritual growth.

When The Star shows up in a Tarot reading, it is vital for you to pay attention to the surrounding cards. The cards that appear alongside The Star can offer further insight into the specific areas of life that are being illuminated. They can provide guidance on the steps to take or the obstacles to overcome in order to truly embrace the transformative energy of this card. If you pulled this card in a single card reading, pull two more to clarify the situation around this card.

In conclusion, The Star is a card that holds a profound message for us as we delve into the art of interpreting Tarot cards. It serves as a reminder of the power of hope, faith, and intuition in our spiritual journeys. By embracing the energy of The Star, students can unlock the mysteries of the Tarot and embark on a transformative path towards self-discovery and enlightenment.

The Moon

If I see the Moon in a reading, I'll say to myself - "Yep, something is being hidden." And that secret will soon be uncovered.

The Moon is an enigmatic card that carries within it a plethora of symbolic meanings, inviting readers and querent to embark on a profound journey of self-discovery and spiritual enlightenment.

The Moon card is the embodiment of the unconscious mind, representing the hidden depths within our psyches. Its presence in a tarot reading urges us to explore our deepest fears, desires, and secrets. This card serves as a reminder that true understanding and growth can only be achieved by delving into the murky waters of the subconscious.

At first glance, The Moon may appear ominous with its dark and mysterious imagery. The moon itself, shrouded in clouds, casts an ethereal glow on a winding path leading into the unknown. Two dogs, one fierce and one gentle, howl at the moon, symbolizing the polarities within our own beings. The crustacean emerging from the water signifies the uncharted territories of our emotions, waiting to be explored.

When The Moon card appears in a tarot reading, it advises us to trust their intuition and embrace the unknown. It serves as a gentle reminder that the path to enlightenment is rarely straightforward or well-lit. The Moon urges us to confront our deepest fears and insecurities, for it is only by facing our shadows that we can truly find balance and harmony.

The Moon represents the cycles of life and the ever-changing nature of existence. It signifies the ebb and flow of our emotions, reminding us that change is inevitable. Just as the moon waxes and wanes, our own experiences and emotions fluctuate, and this card encourages us to embrace this natural rhythm.

To interpret The Moon card, one must tap into their intuition and pay close attention to their dreams and subconscious messages. This card is a call to explore the uncharted territories of our minds and souls, to uncover the hidden knowledge that lies within. By embracing the mysteries of The Moon, we unlock the potential for profound growth and transformation on our spiritual journey.

In conclusion, The Moon card is a powerful and thought-provoking symbol. The Moon invites us to delve into the depths of our unconscious minds, confront our fears, and embrace the ever-changing nature of life. By unlocking the mysteries of The Moon, we embark on a transformative journey, gaining valuable insights into our true selves and the world around us.

The Sun

In the Tarot, few cards hold as much power and positivity as The Sun. Representing illumination, vitality, and enlightenment, The Sun card is a beacon of hope and joy. Knowing this card, The Sun, is essential for unlocking the mysteries of this ancient art.

When The Sun graces a reading, it signifies a time of abundance, success, and achievement. Its radiant energy suggests that all obstacles and challenges will be overcome, and a vibrant new chapter is about to unfold. The Sun is a symbol of clarity and enlightenment, urging us to embrace our inner light and let it shine forth.

In tarot, The Sun card is often associated with personal growth and self-discovery. It encourages us to embrace our true selves, unapologetically basking in our uniqueness. Just as the sun provides warmth and nourishment to all living beings, The Sun card reminds us to radiate positivity and spread joy to those around us. It is a call to embrace our passions and pursue our dreams with unwavering determination.

On a spiritual level, The Sun signifies a deep connection with the divine. It represents the power of the universe, reminding us that we are all interconnected. The Sun's energy encourages us to trust in the greater cosmic plan and have faith in ourselves. It invites us to embrace the present moment and find solace in the beauty of life's simple pleasures.

When interpreting The Sun card, it is important to consider its placement within the spread. As a card of illumination, it can shed light on any situation, providing clarity and guidance. Whether it appears in the past, present, or future position, The Sun card assures us that a period of happiness and fulfillment is on the horizon.

The Sun card is a powerful symbol of optimism and vitality within the card interpretations. Understanding The Sun card is key to unlocking the mysteries of the Tarot. Its radiant energy reminds us to embrace our inner light and let it guide us towards abundance, success, and enlightenment. May The Sun's warmth and positivity illuminate your tarot journey, allowing you to interpret the cards with confidence, insight, and joy.

Judgement

Awakening Your Inner Wisdom

As students of esoteric occult practices, we are constantly seeking to unlock the mysteries that lie within these ancient cards. The Judgement card acts as a powerful catalyst, inviting us to awaken our inner wisdom and embark on a transformative journey of self-discovery.

When this card graces a Tarot reading, it reveals a divine call to reassess our lives, leaving behind the shackles of the past and embracing a future filled with growth and enlightenment. It symbolizes a spiritual awakening, urging us to reflect upon our actions, choices, and the consequences they have had on our journey.

The Judgement card reminds us that we are not mere spectators in our lives, but active participants who possess the power to shape our destinies. It encourages us to take a step back and evaluate the choices we have made, acknowledging the lessons learned and the patterns that have emerged. By doing so, we gain invaluable insights into our true selves and the path that lies ahead.

This card often appears during times of transition, signaling the need for personal growth and transformation. It prompts us to let go of old beliefs, habits, and relationships that no longer serve our higher purpose. The Judgement card embraces the concept of rebirth, urging us to shed our old skin and emerge as the best versions of ourselves.

Interpreting the Judgement card requires deep introspection and a willingness to confront our fears and limitations. It invites us to embark on a journey of self-examination and self-acceptance, encouraging us to listen to the voice of our intuition and trust the guidance of the divine.

Know that the Judgement card holds the key to unlocking our true potential. It reminds us that we are connected to a greater cosmic consciousness and that we have a responsibility to align our actions with the highest good. Through the wisdom gained from interpreting this card, we can tap into our inner reservoir of strength, courage, and compassion, enabling us to navigate life's twists and turns with grace and wisdom.

Embrace the wisdom of the Judgement card and embark on a journey of personal growth, leaving behind the past and embracing a future filled with enlightenment. By interpreting this card with reverence and introspection, we unlock the key to our true potential and align ourselves with the cosmic forces that guide our path.

The World

In the Tarot deck, "The World" card holds immense significance and represents the culmination of a journey. It symbolizes the completion of a cycle and the attainment of ultimate spiritual and personal growth. As you progress in your understanding of Tarot, this card will become a powerful tool for deciphering the mysteries of life.

When "The World" card appears in a reading, it signifies the end of a major phase or project in your life. It suggests that you have reached a state of harmony and balance, having overcome various obstacles and challenges along the way. This card encourages you to celebrate your achievements and embrace the newfound sense of fulfillment.

"The World" also serves as a reminder that everything is connected. It reflects the interplay between different aspects of your life, emphasizing the importance of maintaining harmony between mind, body, and spirit. As above, so below. This card encourages you to embrace unity and recognize the interconnectedness of all things.

Furthermore, "The World" card represents the potential for new beginnings. While it signifies the end of a cycle, it also opens the door to fresh opportunities and ventures. It reminds you that with every ending comes a new beginning, and it is up to you to seize the moment and embark on a new path.

Remember, you possess the power to tap into the energy of "The World" card and use it to manifest your desires. Through meditation, visualization, and intention-setting, you can harness the transformative energy of this card to create positive change in your life and the lives of others.

In conclusion, "The World" card is a profound symbol of completion, unity, and new beginnings. As you deepen your understanding of Tarot, remember to embrace the wisdom and energy that this card offers.

May it guide you on your spiritual journey, empowering you to unlock the mysteries of life and interpret Tarot cards with clarity and insight.

Next up, I'll go over the rest of the cards, known as the Minor Arcana.

Chapter Six

The Tarot - The Minor Arcana

The Minor Arcana, often referred to as the lesser secrets, complements the Major Arcana in its ability to provide detailed insights into the everyday aspects of our lives. Consisting of four suits - Wands, Cups, Swords, and Pentacles - each card within the Minor Arcana carries its own unique symbolism and energy. These cards are deeply intertwined with the elements and astrological correspondences, allowing us to delve into the intricacies of our experiences.

Tarot card readers will find themselves captivated by the intricate stories woven within the Minor Arcana. Whether it be the fiery passion of the Wands, the emotional depths of the Cups, the intellectual prowess of the Swords, or the material abundance of the Pentacles, these cards offer a window into the multifaceted nature of human existence.

Through careful study and practice, you can unlock the profound messages hidden within these cards, offering guidance and clarity in various aspects of life.

For those with an eye for astrology and horoscope analysis, the Minor Arcana can serve as a valuable tool for understanding the influence of celestial bodies in our lives. Each suit corresponds to a specific astrological element, further enhancing our understanding of the cards' meanings. By combining the wisdom of astrology with the insights provided by the Minor Arcana, we can develop a more comprehensive understanding of the energies at play in our lives and how they shape our destinies.

Beyond Tarot cards and astrology, the Minor Arcana also offers a gateway to explore other divination techniques and practices. Whether it is scrying, pendulum dowsing, or any other method, the Minor Arcana can be integrated into these practices to deepen our understanding and enhance our divinatory abilities. By incorporating the symbolism and energy of the cards into our chosen divination techniques, we open ourselves to a world of possibilities and expand our ability to interpret the signs and symbols that surround us.

The Minor Arcana is a treasure trove of wisdom, waiting to be explored by high magic students. It holds the key to understanding the intricacies of Tarot card reading and interpretation, astrology and horoscope analysis, as well as various divination techniques and practices. By immersing ourselves in the knowledge and symbolism of the Minor Arcana, we unlock the potential to become skilled diviners, capable of unraveling the mysteries of the universe and guiding others on their spiritual journeys.

Understanding the Four Suits: Wands, Cups, Swords, and Pentacles

The Minor Arcana, which is an important component of tarot card readings, is divided into four suits, each representing a specific aspect of life and human experience. These suits, namely Wands, Cups, Swords, and Pentacles, hold profound symbolism and offer profound insights into the mysteries of the universe. Our understanding and clairvoyance abilities can be greatly improved by studying the importance of these suits.

The suit of Wands embodies the element of fire, representing passion, creativity, and ambition. It symbolizes the spark of inspiration and the drive to manifest our desires. Wands cards often depict scenes of growth, adventure, and discovery, urging us to embrace our inner fire and take action towards our goals.

Moving on to the suit of Cups, we encounter the element of water, which corresponds to emotions, love, and intuition. This suit deep dives into the vast ocean of our feelings and relationships, offering insights into matters of the heart. From profound love to deep sorrow, Cups cards guide us in understanding our emotional landscapes and encourage us to listen to the whispers of our intuition.

The third suit, Swords, is associated with the element of air, representing intellect, communication, and conflict. Swords cards cut through illusions and reveal the truth, often challenging our preconceptions and calling for clear thinking and honest communication.

This suit reminds us to use our intellect wisely and to confront conflicts with integrity and diplomacy.

Lastly, we explore the suit of Pentacles, embodying the element of earth, symbolizing material possessions, wealth, and physical well-being. This suit focuses on our material world, offering guidance on matters of money, career, and physical health. Pentacles cards remind us of the importance of grounding ourselves and cultivating a solid foundation for a prosperous and abundant life.

By understanding the four suits, we unlock a gateway to the mysteries of tarot. Each suit holds unique energies and messages, reflecting different aspects of our human experience. As seekers of wisdom, interpreting tarot cards becomes a profound and transformative journey, allowing us to tap into the universal consciousness and gain deeper insights into our own lives.

Through diligent study and practice, we can become adept at deciphering the language of tarot, harnessing its ancient wisdom to guide ourselves and others on the path of self- discovery. So let us embark on this enchanting journey into the four suits, embracing the magic that tarot holds and unlocking the mysteries that lie within.

Ace to Ten: Interpretation of Numerical Cards

The numerical cards in Tarot hold a special significance that is imperative to consider when interpreting the cards. These cards serve as the foundation for the Tarot deck, providing valuable insights and messages to anyone who wishes to unravel the mysteries they contain. Our focus in this specific section is to delve deeply into the Ace to Ten cards, expounding upon their interpretation and unlocking the many layers of meaning that they conceal. Our aim is to reveal the hidden magic that lies within these cards and to bring greater clarity to their significance.

The journey begins with the Ace, representing the purest form of its respective suit. It signifies new beginnings, fresh opportunities, and the potential for growth. As students of high magik, we must embrace the essence of the Ace, harnessing its energy to embark on our own transformative paths.

Moving forward, the Two to Ten cards in each suit

reveal the progression of energy and experiences within the realms they represent. The Two symbolizes duality, choices, and partnerships, while the Three signifies creativity, expansion, and collaboration. As we ascend through the ranks, we encounter the Four, embodying stability, structure, and foundation, followed by the Five, representing challenges, conflicts, and change.

The Six card exudes harmony, balance, and resolution, reminding us to find equilibrium in our lives. The Seven brings forth introspection, inner search, and spiritual growth, inviting us to delve deeper into our souls. The Eight symbolizes power, abundance, and achievement, reminding us to embrace our inner strength and manifest our desires. The Nine signifies fulfillment, culmination, and completion, urging us to reflect on our journey and celebrate our achievements.

Lastly, the Ten card serves as the ultimate card of manifestation, representing the culmination of the suit's energy. It signifies abundance, fulfillment, and a sense of wholeness. As students of high magik, we must understand that the Ten card is a testament to our power to manifest our desires, reminding us that we possess the ability to create our own reality.

Interpreting the numerical cards requires a deep understanding of their individual meanings, as well as their relationships with other cards in a spread. Each number carries its unique energy, which is further influenced by the suit it belongs to. By studying and meditating on these cards, we can unlock the secrets of the Tarot, gaining insight into our lives, relationships, and spiritual growth.

In conclusion, the Ace to Ten cards in Tarot hold profound wisdom and symbolism. They guide us on our journey towards self-discovery and spiritual enlightenment. As students of high magik, we must embrace the power within these numerical cards, using them as tools to unlock the mysteries of the Tarot and interpret the messages that lie within.

Court Cards: Pages, Knights, Queens, and Kings

The Court Cards also hold a significant place, representing the various personalities and archetypes that inhabit the spiritual and mystical world. These powerful cards, including Pages, Knights, Queens, and Kings, are essential to unlocking the mysteries that lie within the Tarot deck. It is crucial for us to delve into the rich symbolism and meanings associated with these Court Cards.

The Pages, also known as Princesses, are the messengers of the Tarot deck. They embody youth, curiosity, and the potential for growth. When a Page appears in a reading, it signifies the arrival of new opportunities and fresh perspectives. These cards encourage us to embrace our inner child, to be open-minded and receptive to the possibilities that lie ahead.

The Knights represent action, courage, and ambition. They are the warriors of the Tarot, charging forward fearlessly to conquer challenges and achieve their goals. When a Knight appears in a reading, it signifies the need for assertiveness and taking decisive action. These cards remind us to channel our energy and passion into pursuing our dreams and overcoming obstacles.

The Queens embody feminine energy, nurturing, and intuition. They are the compassionate and wise rulers of the Tarot, offering guidance and support. When a Queen appears in a reading, it signifies the need for self-care, introspection, and emotional balance. These cards urge us to tap into our intuition, trust our instincts, and embrace our nurturing side.

Lastly, the Kings symbolize authority, leadership, and mastery. They are the wise and powerful rulers of the Tarot, representing strength, stability, and responsibility. When a King appears in a reading, it signifies the need for confidence, self-assurance, and taking charge of one's life. These cards remind us to embrace our own inner power and to be assertive in our decision-making.

I have some summary interpretations of each card in

the Reference Manual at the back of this book. I kept it to the more classic interpretations, just to save space in this book. I encourage you to buy the books I mention under "Further Reading".

Chapter Seven

Tarot Spreads

It's very important in our use of the tarot to understand and utilize different tarot spreads. These tarot spreads are specific arrangements of cards that allow the reader to explore different aspects of a querent's life, provide insights, and unveil hidden truths. In this section, I'll take a fast look at the various tarot spreads that will broaden your understanding and enhance your tarot card reading and interpretation skills.

One popular spread is the Celtic Cross, which offers a comprehensive view of the querent's current situation, challenges, and potential outcomes. It consists of ten cards, each representing different aspects of the querent's life, such as relationships, career, and spirituality. By examining the position and interaction of these cards, the tarot reader can gain valuable insights into the querent's life journey.

The Three-Card Spread is perfect for quick, focused readings. Each card represents the past, present, and future, enabling the reader to provide concise guidance on a specific issue or question. This spread is particularly useful for astrology and horoscope analysis enthusiasts who wish to incorporate tarot into their divination practices.

For those seeking to understand the dynamic energies between individuals or explore relationship dynamics, the Relationship Spread is a powerful tool. This spread uses multiple cards to examine each person's perspective, desires, and potential outcomes, offering valuable insights into the strengths and challenges of the relationship.

Furthermore, the Horseshoe Spread provides a comprehensive analysis of a specific situation or problem. With seven cards arranged in the shape of a horseshoe, this spread explores the past, present, and future influences, as well as potential outcomes and advice for the querent.

My favorite spread is all my own. I call it a fast peek at the past, the present, and the future. It uses nine cards, and you start by placing three cards across the top, then three below, and finally three below that. Read each card in the relationship to which row it appears in. Look at the general pattern, and this will give you quick insight into the situation and how to advise your client or yourself.

Lastly, the Zodiac Spread combines tarot card reading with astrology, making it a favorite among high magic students who possess a deep fascination for both divination techniques. Each card represents a sign of the zodiac, offering valuable insights into the querent's personality traits and potential challenges they may face.

Mastering these different tarot spreads will not only enhance your tarot card reading and interpretation skills, but also allow you to explore the intricate connections between astrology, horoscope analysis, and various divination techniques. As a high magic student, incorporating these spreads into your practice will unlock new levels of understanding and enable you to provide profound guidance to those seeking answers and insights through the mystical world of tarot.

Before addressing the spreads, I'll take a few words here to tell you how I do a reading with the cards. As you learn, you will develop your own methods. All the books go into detail about how to shuffle or deal the cards, and they all work.

My technique is to shuffle using a poker shuffle, or riffle shuffle. Split the deck in half. Hold half of the deck lengthwise in your right hand and hold the other half of the deck lengthwise in your left hand. Grip both halves of the deck. Each hand should follow the same position. To grip each half of the deck, place your thumb over the top edge and use your middle and ring fingers to support the bottom edge. Place your pinky finger on the back edge of the deck. Your index finger can go on the front edge or it can hover over the deck for support.

Gently bend each half of the deck. Use your thumbs, index finger, and hands to bend each half of the deck a bit so it becomes concave, with the middle of each deck bending inwards. (This can be difficult with larger cards and new decks, which is why I suggest you shuffle a new deck over and over, until the slick surfaces are roughed up to make shuffling a bit easier.) Riffle the deck with your thumbs. Bend the half-decks back a bit more and use your thumbs to move slowly up the edge of the cards. The cards in the two halves of the decks should riffle together, creating a shuffled deck.

After shuffling a few times, I'll start shuffling again while pondering the question. The first shuffle is when I'll reset the card's energies, allowing them to pick up the new energy around the question.

After this, the cards are ready. I'll also do a cut into three piles, and peek at the cards on the bottom, as a way of checking the energy of the deck. Many people, and I am one of them, will record the cut cards. To do this, cut the deck into three piles, and when picking them back up, make sure the "bottom" pile is now on top.

Other methods of shuffling include simply mixing the deck on the table, an overhand shuffle, plus more. Do a fast search to cover these methods. There are often useful videos.

When shuffling, try to avoid stray thoughts that are off-topic of the question. When reading someone in person, have them shuffle the cards, drawing into the cards their own energy.

Many of these spreads use a card called the "Significator", which represents the person asking the question. For myself, I'll pick the Magician. Otherwise, choose a court card, Queen, King, or Knight, that most resembles the querent.

King and Queen cards represent males and females who are mature or married. The Knight is the symbol of youth between the ages of 18 and 30 and the Pages can be youth or children.

Wands and cups for people with fair hair. Swords for fair skin, dark hair, and pentacles for people with both dark hair and skin colors.

The Celtic Cross Spread

The Celtic Cross Spread is a powerful and versatile

divination technique that has been used for centuries by spiritual practitioners and tarot readers alike. I figure most new tarot readers turn to this spread more than any other spread. So, let's take a look at the intricacies of this spread, its history, and how to interpret its unique patterns to gain valuable insights into the various aspects of life.

Originating from the ancient Celtic druids, the Celtic Cross Spread is a widely respected and trusted divination method. It consists of ten cards arranged in a specific pattern, representing different facets of the querent's life and the energies surrounding them. This spread is popular among magik students, tarot card readers, astrology enthusiasts, and those interested in various divination techniques like scrying and pendulum dowsing.

The first card in the Celtic Cross Spread represents the present situation, providing a snapshot of the querent's current circumstances. Moving clockwise, subsequent cards reveal the past influences, future possibilities, and hidden aspects of the situation. The fifth card, known as the cross, represents the conscious or unconscious forces at play, while the sixth card sheds light on the immediate future.

The seventh card offers guidance on how to approach the situation, serving as a valuable tool for decision-making. Next, the eighth card represents the querent's external influences, such as friends, family, or external circumstances. Then the ninth card reveals the querent's hopes and fears, providing insight into their emotional state. Finally, the tenth card, commonly known as the outcome card, reveals the potential outcome of the situation.

Interpreting the Celtic Cross Spread requires a deep understanding of the symbolic meanings of each card, as well as intuition and psychic abilities. The position of each card in the spread provides context and adds layers of meaning. For instance, a card in a past position may show a past event or influence that has shaped the present situation.

By mastering the Celtic Cross Spread, high magic students can unlock a wealth of knowledge and gain profound insights into the lives of their clients. Whether you are a tarot card reader, an astrology enthusiast, or someone interested in divination techniques, the Celtic Cross Spread is a valuable tool in your spiritual journey.

Remember, the key to mastering this technique lies in practice, intuition, and a deep connection to the spiritual realm.

The Three-Card Spread

Among the various spreads used in tarot, the Three-Card Spread stands out as a simple yet powerful tool for gaining quick and insightful answers to specific questions.

My nine-card spread expands on this simple spread.

Astrology and horoscope analysis enthusiasts, as well as those interested in divination techniques and practices like scrying and pendulum dowsing, will find the Three-Card Spread a valuable addition to their repertoire. This spread allows practitioners to focus their energy on a particular query and obtain concise guidance.

To perform the Three-Card Spread, start by shuffling your tarot deck while concentrating on your question. Once you feel ready, draw three cards and arrange them in a horizontal line, face down. Each card represents an aspect of the question at hand: past, present, and future.

When ready, turn over the first card, which reveals the past influences related to the query. This card offers insights into the circumstances that have shaped the situation, providing a foundation for understanding the present and future aspects. Pay attention to symbols, colors, and the card's overall message to decipher its meaning.

Moving on to the middle card, this represents the present situation. It offers guidance on the current state of affairs and provides a glimpse into the energies surrounding the question.

Dive deep into its symbolism, as it holds the key to understanding the dynamics at play in the present moment.

Finally, unveil the third card, which uncovers the

future outcome or potential path. This card acts as a guiding light, providing valuable information on the probable trajectory of the situation. Interpret the card's symbolism while considering the context of the past and present cards to gain a comprehensive understanding of the potential outcome.

Remember, the Three-Card Spread is merely a tool to help uncover hidden insights and possibilities. It is essential to trust your intuition and cultivate a connection with the cards as you interpret their messages. With practice, this spread can become a reliable means of exploring the depths of the unknown and finding clarity in the mystical realms.

The Relationship Spread

The Relationship Spread holds a special place for those seeking answers and guidance in matters of the heart. Whether you are a seasoned tarot card reader, an astrology enthusiast, or a curious practitioner of various divination techniques, this section will delve into the intricacies of the Relationship Spread, offering insights and techniques to unlock its hidden wisdom.

Tarot card reading and interpretation have long been cherished methods of understanding and unraveling the complexities of relationships. The Relationship Spread, consisting of multiple cards carefully laid out, provides a profound glimpse into the dynamics between individuals. Each card represents an aspect of the relationship, shedding light on its strengths, challenges, and potential outcomes. As a high magic student, mastering the art of interpreting the cards' symbolism and their interplay is vital in providing accurate and meaningful readings to your clients.

Astrology and horoscope analysis also have much to offer when exploring relationships. By examining the planetary positions at the time of birth, astrologers can discern the compatibility and potential challenges between partners. The Relationship Spread in astrology involves analyzing the natal charts of both individuals and identifying the aspects and planetary placements that influence their connection. This section will guide you through the intricate process of deciphering these celestial messages and empowering you to provide valuable insights to those seeking astrological guidance.

Additionally, this chapter will touch upon various divination techniques and practices that can be applied to the Relationship Spread. Scrying, for instance, allows the diviner to tap into their intuitive abilities and gain insights into the hidden dynamics of a relationship. Pendulum dowsing, on the other hand, provides a simple yet effective way of receiving answers to specific questions related to relationships. Exploring these techniques and their applications in the context of relationships will expand your divinatory toolkit and offer unique perspectives to your clients.

To begin, you will shuffle the cards, or have the querent shuffle the cards. After cutting the deck, as described earlier, lay seven cards out. I do three across the top, one in the center, then three across the bottom. Read the cards in relationship to the card number in the layout.

1. **Your wants** - What are you looking for in a relationship? What do you need from the relationship to consider it successful?
2. **Partner's wants** - What does your partner want in a relationship? What would they need for it to be successful?
3. **Differences** - In what parts of life do you two find differences? What are possible points of disagreement?
4. **Similarities** - Where in life do you find similarities? What brings you together?
5. **Emotional Compatibility** - How compatible are you emotionally?
6. **Physical Compatibility** - How compatible are you physically? How would you characterize your physical relationship?
7. **Mental Compatibility** - How compatible are you mentally? Do you find similar things to be intellectually stimulating?

Relationship spreads vary. You will find books filled with various spreads for relationships, so use this section as just a starting spot. I encourage you to develop your own spreads, using this as a starting spot. Whether your clients seek answers about romantic partnerships, friendships, or family dynamics, mastering the art of the Relationship Spread will empower you to provide accurate, compassionate, and transformative readings. This section is your guide to unlocking the profound wisdom embedded in the cards, the stars, and the various divination techniques, and helping others navigate the labyrinth of relationships with clarity and insight.

Chapter Eight

My History with Astrology

In 1990, I found this huge, red book about astrology. After going over it, and collecting data on myself and my then-wife, I began casting our charts.

What was amazing, my progression chart for my wife indicated that not only would she be pregnant, she'd also be hospitalized for a lengthy time.

Turned out, that within a month, yes, we had a baby on the way. Then she spent five or so weeks in the hospital in Austin because within two weeks of moving to Austin, she started labor about nine weeks early.

Later on, I ditched the dusty ephemeris books for a computer program, no more hunting for the current alignments, making the (easily miscalculated) time adjustments for my time zone, no more wondering if I had the correct figures, a program just went to work, and pulled the chart together in a blink of an eye.

If you wish real accuracy, you will need to delve into the natal charts, or progressed charts, which are the only real way to get an accurate astrology

Astrology and Magik

Some magik systems need, or require, you to perform specific rituals during specific astrological times. Specifically, candle magik requires that you work either during the New to Full cycle (bring) or Full to New cycle (release).

I'll focus more on the use of Astrology in divination, versus trying to go over the tedious and mind-numbing process of casting natal charts, progression charts, and the like, seeing as how there's a lot of good programs and apps to do this for you.

However, our focus will shift towards the utilization of Astrology in divination work. Yes, a progressed chart will help you out a lot, and as I have said, when I did a detailed progressed chart by hand, I was really accurate. This is not just a coincidence; it is accurate beyond mere chance.

I'll simply summarize each astrological sign and astrological houses, then go into the use of astrology as it relates to divination briefly. Going in depth is beyond the scope of this book, as it appears that this book will be quite thick already, thus adding in-depth info about astrology in general will make this book even bigger. I will mention transits, of course, but instead of going over the process of calculating these transits, find a decent program to calculate all this for you. I'm a big proponent of using the computer, or web, to handle the tedious processes we used to do by hand (such as writing a book!)

It is important to note that a vast majority of the software options available on the market are quite expensive, so keep that in mind. If you intend to offer astrological services to clients, then make the investment. Otherwise, find and use the free websites - of which there are a multitude.

A Summary of the History of Astrology

Astrology is an ancient belief system that suggests a connection between the positions and movements of celestial bodies, such as planets and stars, and events on Earth, including human lives and natural phenomena. It has a long and complex history that spans across various cultures and civilizations.

The origins of astrology can be traced back to ancient Mesopotamia, around 2,000 BCE. Babylonian astronomers began observing and recording the movements of celestial bodies and correlating them with events on Earth. This early form of astrology, known as mundane astrology, focused on predicting natural disasters and the fate of nations.

As cultures interacted and exchanged knowledge, astrology spread to ancient Egypt, Greece, and eventually to the Roman Empire. In ancient Greece, figures like Ptolemy contributed significantly to the development of astrology. The Hellenistic period saw the emergence of horoscopic astrology, which placed emphasis on the positions of celestial bodies at the exact moment of a person's birth to create a birth chart or horoscope. This chart was believed to provide insights into an individual's personality, life events, and potential.

During the Islamic Golden Age, scholars in the Islamic world further developed astrology. They translated Greek and Babylonian texts and incorporated their own insights, contributing to the refinement of astrological techniques. Astrology continued to evolve through the Middle Ages in Europe, with Christian and Jewish scholars engaging with its concepts.

The Renaissance marked a revival of interest in astrology, as thinkers sought to reconcile it with emerging scientific knowledge. However, as the scientific method gained prominence, astrology began to face criticism and skepticism. The Age of Enlightenment saw a decline in astrology's status, as it was often regarded as superstitious and lacking empirical evidence.

Despite its challenges, astrology persisted and adapted to modern times. In the 20th century, psychological astrology emerged, focusing on personal growth and introspection rather than prediction. With the rise of the New Age movement, astrology regained popularity as part of a broader interest in spirituality and self-discovery.

Today, astrology exists in various forms, from traditional horoscopic astrology to more specialized branches, like medical astrology or financial astrology. It continues to have a presence in popular culture and is practiced by individuals seeking guidance, insight, or a connection to cosmic forces.

Astrology eventually led to astronomy. Astronomy shouldn't be confused with Astrology, however. It's a fast way to get a science minded individual to roll their eyes and emit a long sigh. I've seen this happen in college astronomy courses, as young people would leave and ask to drop the astronomy class, thinking they'd signed up for an astrology course.

As far as casting your own charts, I recommend not checking out multiple large books on the subject, including an updated ephemeris, but use an astrology program. There are multiple programs now, and the one(s) I used are not compatible with current systems. So, I usually go online if I need to generate a natal chart or progressed chart.

Chapter Nine

Exploring the Zodiac Signs

The Zodiac Signs are a fundamental aspect of astrology and horoscope analysis. They represent different personalities, characteristics, and life paths based on the position of the Sun at the time of birth. As high magic students, you understand the significance of energy and how it influences our lives. The Zodiac Signs act as a map, guiding us to explore the unique energies that govern our existence.

By examining each Zodiac Sign, you will learn about their ruling planet, element, and modality. Discover how Aries embodies the fiery spirit of initiation, while Taurus invokes stability and earthly pleasures. Explore the duality of Gemini, the nurturing nature of Cancer, and the regal charisma of Leo. Unveil the analytical mind of Virgo, the balanced diplomacy of Libra, and the passionate intensity of Scorpio. Unearth the adventurous spirit of Sagittarius, the disciplined ambition of Capricorn, and the innovative intellect of Aquarius. Finally, immerse yourself in the compassionate empathy of Pisces.

To further enrich your divination practices, we will also explore how each Zodiac Sign interacts with tarot card reading and interpretation. The Tarot deck is a powerful tool that can provide guidance, insight, and answers to life's most pressing questions.

Understanding the connection between the Zodiac Signs and the Tarot cards will allow you to refine your readings and offer more accurate interpretations.

Additionally, we will explore a range of divination techniques and practices that are in harmony with the Zodiac Signs. No matter what type of divination you practice, whether it be scrying, pendulum dowsing, or any other form, adding the understanding of the Zodiac Signs to your practice will greatly enhance your abilities. By understanding how each sign influences divination practices, you can learn how to harness their energies for more profound and accurate readings, making your practice even more successful.

Embrace the ancient wisdom and hidden knowledge they hold. By exploring their mysteries, you will unlock new levels of insight, intuition, and divination prowess. May this section be a guiding light on your journey to becoming a master of the high arts, astrology, and ancient divination techniques.

Aries

Aries is the first sign of the zodiac, symbolizing the beginning of a new cycle. As a high magic student with a passion for divination, it is essential to delve into the depths of Aries's energy and understand its influence on tarot card reading, astrology, and various divination techniques.

Tarot Card Reading and Interpretation: Aries, represented by the ram, embodies qualities of enthusiasm, courage, and assertiveness. When exploring tarot cards, its fiery nature can be seen in cards such as The Emperor, The Chariot, and The Tower. The Emperor signifies leadership and control, reflecting Aries's natural tendency to take charge. The Chariot symbolizes determination and victory, reflecting Aries's drive to overcome obstacles. The Tower represents sudden change and upheaval, reflecting Aries's impulsive and sometimes confrontational nature. Understanding these cards in relation to Aries can enhance your tarot interpretations and provide deeper insights into your readings.

Astrology and Horoscope Analysis:

Aries, ruled by Mars, is a sign known for its pioneering spirit and boldness. People born under this sign are often independent, energetic, and adventurous. Studying Aries in astrology can help you gain a profound understanding of the personality traits associated with this sign. By analyzing Aries in birth charts, you can explore the influence of Mars on different aspects of life, such as career, relationships, and personal growth. Understanding Aries's compatibility with other signs can provide valuable insights for astrology practitioners seeking to deepen their knowledge of relationship dynamics.

Divination Techniques and Practices:

Aries's energy can also be harnessed in various divination techniques to enhance your practice. For scrying, the assertiveness and fearlessness of Aries can help you focus your gaze and receive clearer visions. Pendulum dowsing can benefit from Aries's decisive nature, allowing you to ask direct questions and receive concise answers. By invoking Aries's passionate energy during divination rituals, you can infuse your practice with determination and confidence, ultimately leading to more accurate and insightful readings.

By understanding its influence on various aspects of

divination, you can deepen your practice and provide more profound readings to those seeking guidance. Embrace the fiery spirit of Aries and let it guide you towards unlocking the secrets of the ancient divination arts.

Taurus: Unveiling the Secrets of the Bull

We now turn our attention to the enigmatic zodiac sign of Taurus, a symbol of strength, stability, and sensuality. Embark on a journey through the realms of Tarot card reading, astrology, and other divination practices as we unravel the secrets of the Bull.

Tarot Card Reading and Interpretation: In the realm of Tarot card reading, Taurus embodies the energy of the Hierophant.

Representing tradition, wisdom, and spiritual growth, this card encourages introspection and the exploration of deep-rooted beliefs.

Learn to interpret the Hierophant's presence in a spread, uncovering the significance of its symbolism and how it influences the seeker's path. Delve into the Bull's connection to the Major Arcana cards, such as the Empress and the Devil, to discern the hidden messages and advice they hold.

Astrology and Horoscope Analysis:

Astrology enthusiasts, rejoice! As we delve into Taurus, we explore the celestial influences that shape this fixed earth sign. Learn how the positioning of Venus, Taurus' ruling planet, impacts their sensuality, love life, and creative expression. Discover the compatibility between Taurus and other signs, unlocking the mysteries of their relationships. Dive into the Taurus horoscope, uncovering the astrological predictions and guidance that await those born under this sign.

Divination Techniques and Practices:

Delve deeper into the world of divination techniques with a focus on Taurus. Explore scrying, a practice involving gazing into reflective surfaces to access hidden knowledge. Learn the art of pendulum dowsing and how a Taurus' innate stability and groundedness can enhance their accuracy.

Discover the unique abilities and strengths Taurus possesses in various divination practices, harnessing their patience and determination to unveil hidden truths.

By delving into the essence of Taurus, you will gain a profound understanding of this zodiac sign's energy and how it intertwines with the mystical arts.

Whether you are a Tarot card reader, astrology enthusiast, or divination practitioner, this section offers a comprehensive exploration of the Bull's secrets. Expand your knowledge, refine your skills, and unlock the ancient wisdom that lies within the Taurus archetype.

Gemini: The Enigmatic Twins of the Zodiac

In the vast tapestry of the celestial realm, each zodiac sign holds a unique position, offering distinct insight into the mysteries of the Universe. Among these enigmatic signs, Gemini stands as a beacon of duality and versatility. As high magic students, delving into the realms of tarot card reading, astrology, and various divination practices, understanding the essence of Gemini is crucial for unlocking hidden knowledge and harnessing its power.

Tarot Card Reading and Interpretation:

Within the realm of tarot, the Gemini energy is embodied by the Lovers card, symbolizing the duality of choices and the constant search for balance. The card invites us to embrace the Gemini's gift of adaptability, encouraging us to explore different paths and perspectives.

When interpreting the Lovers card, pay close attention to the interplay between the two figures, representing the dual nature of Gemini and the importance of harmonizing opposing forces.

Astrology and Horoscope Analysis:

For astrology enthusiasts, Gemini is ruled by the planet Mercury, bestowing upon it quick wit, eloquence, and a profound affinity for communication. Geminis are known for their sharp intellect, versatility, and love for social interactions. Analyzing a Gemini's birth chart will shed light on their unique blend of air and mutable qualities, indicating their ability to effortlessly adapt to changing circumstances and their insatiable thirst for knowledge.

Divination Techniques and Practices:

When it comes to divination, Geminis are known to possess a natural talent for intuitive practices such as scrying and pendulum dowsing. Their dual nature enables them to bridge the gap between the conscious and unconscious, making them exceptional at interpreting signs, symbols, and omens. As students, exploring these divination techniques under the guidance of Gemini's influence will amplify your abilities to decipher hidden messages from the Universe.

However, it is important to note that the Gemini's dualistic nature can sometimes lead to indecisiveness or superficiality. To harness the true potential of Gemini's influence, one must cultivate focus, grounding, and discernment. Engaging in meditative practices, such as mindfulness or yoga, will aid in balancing the mercurial energies and achieving clarity amidst the constant flux.

Embrace the multifaceted nature of the twins, harness their adaptability, and discover the hidden realms that await your exploration. The Gemini energy will guide you through the realms of duality, communication, and the art of deciphering hidden truths.

Cancer: The Mystical Insights

The study of Cancer extends far beyond its conventional medical definition. Cancer, as a celestial sign and an ancient divination technique, holds deep mystical insights that can greatly enrich the practices of tarot card reading and interpretation, astrology and horoscope analysis, as well as various divination techniques and practices like scrying and pendulum dowsing.

To the people who are eager to expand their knowledge, Cancer is not merely a zodiac sign. It represents the nurturing and intuitive qualities of the divine feminine energy, deeply connected to the element of water. Within the realm of tarot card reading, Cancer enhances the interpretation of cards associated with emotions, intuition, and family matters. Understanding the Cancerian archetype allows the reader to tap into the emotional depths of the querent, providing profound insights into their inner world.

Astrology enthusiasts will find Cancer to be a treasure trove of wisdom. This cardinal water sign rules the moon, symbolizing the ebb and flow of emotions, the subconscious, and the nurturing aspects of our lives. By exploring the unique characteristics of Cancer in birth charts and horoscope analysis, astrologers can unravel hidden patterns and gain a deeper understanding of individuals' emotional needs and family dynamics.

As the moon passes through various phases, so do Cancers. In my mind, Cancers are also tied to the power and magik of the triple-moon goddess, Hecate. Some may wish to argue against this, but my assessment is based upon my lifelong association with various people who were born under this sign.

For those practicing divination techniques and practices, Cancer offers a gateway to connect with the ethereal realms. Scrying, the ancient art of gazing into reflective surfaces to perceive messages from the spirit world, finds resonance with Cancer's intuitive nature.

Pendulum dowsing, the use of a suspended object to receive answers from the divine, becomes more potent when aligned with Cancer's ability to tap into the subconscious mind.

By embracing the wisdom of this mystical sign, you will attain a deeper understanding of your clients, enhance your divinatory skills, and forge a profound connection with the unseen forces that shape our lives.

Embark on a journey of self-discovery and mystical exploration as you delve into the secrets of Cancer. May this section be your guide in unlocking the hidden potentials of tarot card reading, astrology, and various divination techniques, ultimately enriching your path as a high magic student.

Leo

In the realm of ancient divination techniques, the zodiac sign Leo holds a significant place. As an high magic student, it is crucial to delve deep into the mysteries of Leo, as it can provide valuable insights into our lives, personalities, and future paths. In this section, we will explore the profound connection between Leo and various divination practices, including tarot card reading and interpretation, astrology and horoscope analysis, as well as divination techniques such as scrying and pendulum dowsing.

Tarot Card Reading and Interpretation:
Leo, ruled by the Sun, is associated with the Strength

card in the tarot deck. This card represents courage, vitality, and the ability to overcome challenges. When this card appears in a reading, it signifies Leo's dominant traits in the seeker's life. It encourages them to embrace their inner strength, stand tall, and assert themselves in all aspects of life.

Astrology and Horoscope Analysis:

As the fifth sign of the zodiac, Leo is known for its fiery energy and leadership qualities.

Individuals born under this sign are often charismatic, confident, and passionate.

Astrologers analyze the position of the Sun, Moon, and other celestial bodies at the time of birth to provide accurate horoscopes for Leo individuals. These horoscopes shed light on various aspects of their lives, including relationships, career, and personal growth.

Divination Techniques and Practices:

Leo's connection with divination goes beyond tarot and astrology. Scrying, a divination technique involving gazing into a reflective surface, can be particularly powerful for Leo individuals. By tapping into their natural ability to connect with their intuition, Leos can receive profound insights and guidance through scrying.

Pendulum dowsing is another divination method that Leos can explore. By harnessing their strong sense of self and determination, Leo individuals can use a pendulum to seek answers to questions, as the pendulum's movements can be interpreted as divine guidance.

In conclusion, delving into the mysteries of Leo is essential for all students of the occult and esoteric practices, especially those interested in tarot card reading and interpretation, astrology and horoscope analysis, and various divination techniques such as scrying and pendulum dowsing. By understanding the unique traits and energies associated with Leo, high magic students can enhance their divination practices and gain deeper insights into themselves and the world around them.

Virgo

The Meticulous Maiden

Meticulous, yes, maiden probably not.

Time to take a look at the Virgos. Stereotyped as fussy people, being a Virgo myself, and looking around my workspace, I see little of the fussiness associated with Virgos. I have a lot of clutter scattered about my various work spaces, but I know where everything is.

In astrology and horoscope analysis, Virgo is the

sixth sign of the zodiac, ruled by the planet Mercury. Known for their analytical minds, practicality, and attention to detail, Virgos possess a natural affinity for divination techniques and practices. They are the seekers of truth, constantly striving for perfection in all aspects of their lives.

Tarot card reading and interpretation are particularly well-suited for Virgos. With their innate ability to analyze situations and pay attention to the smallest details, they excel at unraveling the hidden meanings within the cards. Their meticulous nature enables them to provide accurate readings, offering valuable insights and guidance to those seeking answers.

Astrology plays a significant role in understanding Virgo's personality traits and divination abilities. By analyzing the Virgo birth chart, high magic students can uncover the unique strengths and weaknesses of individuals born under this sign. This knowledge can enhance their divination practices and tailor readings to suit the specific needs of Virgo clients.

Divination techniques and practices such as scrying and pendulum dowsing can be powerful tools in a Virgo's arsenal. Their sharp minds and attention to detail allow them to focus deeply on scrying mediums or interpret the subtle movements of a pendulum.

Through these methods, Virgos can tap into their

inner wisdom and connect with higher realms to seek answers and guidance.

However, it is essential for Virgos to balance their meticulous nature with a sense of openness and intuition. Over-analysis can sometimes hinder their divination abilities, blocking the flow of energies. By embracing their intuition and trusting their instincts, Virgos can unlock their full potential as diviners.

By understanding the unique traits of Virgo and harnessing their meticulous nature, you will be able to offer accurate insights and guidance to those seeking divination services. Embrace the meticulous maiden within you and explore the enchanting world of Virgo divination.

Libra

Balancing the Scales of Divination

Libra holds a significant place as the seventh zodiac sign, symbolizing balance, harmony, and justice. As an air sign ruled by Venus, Libra's energy resonates with the delicate art of divination. In this section, we delve into the unique qualities of Libra and explore how they influence the practices of tarot card reading, astrology, and various divination techniques.

Tarot Card Reading and Interpretation:

Libra's influence on tarot card reading is profound, bringing forth the themes of justice, fairness, and diplomacy. As a high magic student, understanding the Libran energy allows you to interpret the cards through the lens of balance and equilibrium. The Justice card, for instance, embodies Libra's essence, guiding you to make fair decisions and seek harmony in all aspects of life. By grasping the interconnectedness of Libra's energy with tarot, you'll uncover new depths in your readings and provide insightful guidance to those seeking balance.

Astrology and Horoscope Analysis:

When exploring astrology and horoscope analysis, the influence of Libra becomes clear through the seventh house, which governs partnerships, relationships, and justice. As an occult student, familiarizing yourself with Libra's energy enhances your ability to interpret birth charts and provide valuable insights into relationship dynamics. The Libra energy encourages you to seek fairness and balance in your astrological interpretations, ensuring that you provide well-rounded and accurate guidance to your clients.

Divination Techniques and Practices:

Libra's influence extends beyond tarot card reading and astrology, infusing divination techniques such as scrying and pendulum dowsing with its unique energy. When practicing scrying, the Libra energy encourages you to seek balance and harmony in the images that arise, guiding you to find equilibrium in your interpretations. Similarly, in pendulum dowsing, Libra's energy aids in uncovering truths and making decisions that align with fairness and justice. By incorporating Libra's influence into your divination practices, you cultivate a deeper connection with the energies at play and provide more comprehensive and insightful readings.

As a high magic student, delving into the Libra energy unlocks a world of balance, harmony, and justice within the realms of tarot card reading, astrology, and divination techniques. By embracing Libra's essence, you'll enhance your ability to interpret symbols, decipher birth charts, and uncover hidden truths. As you navigate the delicate dance of divination, let the scales of Libra guide you towards a deeper understanding of the forces at play, both within yourself and in the world around you.

Scorpio

The Mystical Depths of Transformation

As you delve deeper into astrology, you will undoubtedly encounter the enigmatic and intense energy of Scorpio. I have encountered quite a few women who are under this sign, and it may seem like stereotyping, but yes, they do all seem to fall into the description of a Scorpio!

Represented by the scorpion, this astrological sign holds immense power and mystery that is sure to captivate the hearts and minds of high magic students.

In the section on Scorpio, we will explore the multifaceted aspects of this sign and its significance in various divination practices.

Whether you are a tarot card enthusiast, an astrology aficionado, or an avid practitioner of divination techniques like scrying or pendulum dowsing, Scorpio's profound influence cannot be overlooked.

Tarot card readers will find Scorpio to be an intriguing and complex archetype. The sign's ruling planet, Pluto, is associated with transformation and regeneration. It plunges us into the depths of the subconscious, revealing hidden truths and unearthing buried emotions. The Scorpio tarot cards, such as Death and the Tower, symbolize the transformative power of this sign, urging us to embrace change and let go of what no longer serves us.

Astrology and horoscope analysis enthusiasts will discover that Scorpio brings intensity and passion to any birth chart. Known for their deep emotional connections and profound insights, Scorpios possess an innate ability to uncover secrets and uncover hidden motivations. Their determination and resourcefulness make them natural investigators, seeking out the truth in all aspects of life.

For those interested in divination techniques and practices, Scorpio's energy can be harnessed to enhance your abilities. Scrying, a method of gazing into reflective surfaces to access deeper levels of consciousness, is particularly well-suited to Scorpio's introspective nature. By invoking the transformative energy of Scorpio, you can unlock hidden knowledge and gain profound insights into your own psyche and the world around you.

Pendulum dowsing, another divination practice, can also benefit from Scorpio's influence. By tapping into Scorpio's intense energy, you can channel the power of the subconscious mind and receive accurate and intuitive answers from the pendulum.

Whether you are drawn to tarot card readings, astrology, or divination practices, Scorpio's transformative energy and mystical depths will undoubtedly enrich your understanding and abilities in these fields. Embrace the scorpion's potent energy and embark on a journey of transformation and self-discovery.

Sagittarius

Sagittarius holds a special place as one of the most vibrant and adventurous zodiac signs. Represented by the symbol of the Archer, Sagittarians are known for their love of freedom, exploration, and intellectual pursuits. In this section, we will delve into the mysteries of Sagittarius, exploring its unique characteristics and providing insights for high magic students, particularly those interested in tarot card reading and interpretation, astrology, and various divination techniques.

For tarot card readers, Sagittarius presents an exciting energy to work with. The Sagittarian's optimistic nature and hunger for knowledge are reflected in cards like the Fool, the Wheel of Fortune, and the Chariot. These cards signify a sense of adventure, expansion, and the pursuit of truth. When interpreting these cards, it is essential to tap into the Sagittarian energy and encourage seekers to embrace their curiosity and venture into uncharted territories.

Astrology enthusiasts will find Sagittarius to be a fascinating sign to study. Ruled by Jupiter, the planet of growth and expansion, Sagittarius embodies wisdom, philosophy, and a thirst for spiritual understanding. Exploring the Sagittarian birth chart can reveal the areas of life where one seeks higher meaning and personal growth. Understanding the interactions between Sagittarius and other signs can provide valuable insights into relationships and compatibility.

For those interested in divination techniques and practices, Sagittarius offers a gateway to explore the realms beyond.

Scrying, the ancient art of gazing into reflective surfaces to gain insight, can be enhanced by invoking Sagittarian qualities of intuition and exploration. Pendulum dowsing, another divination method, can benefit from Sagittarius's natural affinity for seeking answers and uncovering hidden truths.

To harness the energies of Sagittarius, high magic students can perform rituals or create altars adorned with symbols associated with this sign. Incorporating elements such as arrows, maps, books, and images of great thinkers can enhance the sacred space and invite Sagittarian energies to guide their practices.

In conclusion, Sagittarius offers a wealth of knowledge and inspiration for high magic students, particularly those interested in tarot card reading, astrology, and various divination techniques. By embracing the Sagittarian spirit of adventure, curiosity, and expansion, students can deepen their understanding of these ancient divination practices and unlock new realms of insight and wisdom. May Sagittarius' arrow guide you on your mystical journey!

Capricorn

Capricorn stands as a celestial sign that captivates the very essence of determination and practicality. As a student delving into the mystical arts, it is vital to grasp the profound influence that Capricorn holds over the cosmic tapestry. In this section, we explore the multifaceted nature of Capricorn, unraveling its significance in various divination techniques, such as tarot card reading, astrology, and other divination practices.

I have personally had multiple relationships with Capricorns, and my daughter is one as well. One trait they all seem to have is a stubbornness streak about half a kilometer wide. I also tend to see them show up in a tarot reading as one of the swords court cards.

Tarot Card Reading and Interpretation:

When encountering the Capricorn card in a tarot deck, it signifies an embodiment of ambition, discipline, and wisdom. The card often portrays a mountain goat scaling the heights, symbolizing the Capricornian determination to overcome obstacles and reach the pinnacle of success. As a high magic student, harnessing the tenacity and dedication exemplified by the Capricorn energy can prove beneficial in your own journey towards enlightenment.

Astrology and Horoscope Analysis:

Capricorn, an earth sign ruled by the disciplined planet Saturn, instills a sense of responsibility and structure in those born under its influence. Individuals with a Capricorn sun sign is often characterized by their steadfastness, organizational skills, and long-term vision. As an astrology enthusiast, understanding the unique traits of Capricorn can aid in deciphering birth charts, enhancing horoscope analysis, and providing valuable insights into the lives of individuals.

Divination Techniques and Practices:

Capricorn's practical nature lends itself well to various divination techniques. For instance, when engaging in scrying, the Capricorn energy can help focus the mind and discern hidden messages within reflective surfaces.

Pendulum dowsing, another divination practice, can benefit from the structured and determined essence of Capricorn, ensuring precise answers to queries.

Furthermore, those seeking guidance from the

celestial realm can call upon the energy of Capricorn during ritualistic practices. By incorporating Capricornian symbols, such as the mountain goat or Saturn's planetary sigil, into spells or rituals, high magic students can harness the grounding and ambitious qualities associated with this sign.

In conclusion, Capricorn's influence in the realms of tarot card reading, astrology, and various divination techniques is undeniable. By delving into the depths of this sign's characteristics, high magic students specializing in tarot card reading and interpretation, astrology and horoscope analysis, as well as divination techniques and practices, can expand their knowledge and refine their craft. Embrace the essence of Capricorn, and unlock the keys to a world of wisdom, determination, and practicality.

Aquarius

The enigmatic realm of Aquarius, a sign that holds a mystical allure for those with an affinity for Tarot card reading and interpretation, astrology and horoscope analysis, as well as various divination techniques and practices.

There's also a catchy late 1960s song, "Age of Aquarius." This song might have triggered my fascination with astrology.

Aquarius, often symbolized by the Water Bearer, is the eleventh sign of the zodiac and is ruled by the planet

Uranus. Those born between January 20th and February 18th are blessed with the Aquarian energy. This sign is characterized by its air element, representing intellect, innovation, and humanitarian tendencies. Aquarians are known for their independent thinking, originality, and progressive mindset. They possess a natural flair for creativity and often excel in fields that require a visionary approach.

For Tarot enthusiasts, the Aquarian energy can be channeled through cards like The Star and The Fool. The Star signifies hope, healing, and inspiration, while The Fool symbolizes new beginnings and embracing the unknown.

When interpreting these cards in a reading, pay attention to the themes of individuality, unconventional thinking, and the pursuit of higher truths, which are intrinsic to Aquarius.

Astrology enthusiasts will find Aquarius to be a captivating sign to explore. Birth charts and horoscopes reveal the unique personality traits, strengths, and challenges of individuals born under this sign. Their ruling planet, Uranus, brings an eccentric and unpredictable energy, emphasizing the importance of embracing change and embracing one's authentic self.

In the realm of divination techniques and practices, Aquarius aligns well with scrying and pendulum dowsing.

Scrying, often conducted with a crystal ball or a black mirror, allows the Aquarian mind to tap into their intuitive abilities and receive messages from the cosmos. Pendulum dowsing, on the other hand, aids in accessing the subconscious mind and uncovering hidden truths.

Incorporate its essence of the Aquarian sun sign into your Tarot readings, astrology readings, and divination practices. Allow the wisdom of this sign to guide you towards innovation, humanitarianism, and the pursuit of higher knowledge. May the celestial forces of Aquarius illuminate your path and inspire your divination endeavors.

Pisces

The Mystical Realm of the Fish

Pisces is the twelfth and final sun sign, and is unique in its ethereal and intuitive nature. It is a realm where dreams and reality intertwine and the boundaries between the seen and unseen become blurred.

For those of you in the niches of tarot card reading and interpretation, astrology and horoscope analysis, and divination techniques and practices, understanding Pisces is crucial. This section will delve into the depths of Pisces' symbolism, its ruling planet, and its influence on divination.

Ruled by Neptune, the planet of intuition, illusion,

and spirituality, Pisces is associated with the element of water. This element signifies the realm of emotions, intuition, and the subconscious mind. Pisces individuals are often deeply sensitive and empathetic, making them natural healers and dreamers. They possess an uncanny ability to tap into unseen energies and connect with the collective consciousness.

In tarot, Pisces is represented by the Moon card, symbolizing the realm of dreams, intuition, and the unconscious mind. When this card appears in a reading, it urges us to trust our inner voice, pay attention to our dreams, and embrace our intuitive nature. It reminds us that sometimes the answers we seek lie beyond the realm of logic and reason.

Astrologically, Pisces governs the twelfth house, the house of the hidden, the spiritual, and the subconscious. It is a domain where deep introspection, meditation, and connection with higher realms are encouraged. As astrologers, understanding the influence of Pisces in a birth chart can provide valuable insights into an individual's spiritual path and potential psychic abilities.

For those practicing various divination techniques, such as scrying or pendulum dowsing, Pisces offers a gateway to explore the vast depths of the unconscious mind. By tapping into the Piscean energy, one can enhance their psychic abilities and access hidden knowledge and spiritual guidance.

In conclusion, Pisces holds a special place in the realm of all manifestation magic. Its intuitive and dreamy nature opens doors to unseen realms and hidden wisdom. By understanding the symbolism, ruling planet, and influence of Pisces, tarot card readers, astrologers, and divination practitioners can deepen their practice and unlock the secrets of the universe. So, embrace the mystical energy of Pisces, and let the fish guide you on a journey of spiritual discovery and divination mastery.

Chapter Ten

Understanding Astrological Houses

You thought I was done after quickly covering the twelve astrological signs? If I'd stopped there, you would be missing out on one of the fundamental components of astrology! I'm talking about the concept of astrological houses. These houses play a crucial role in interpreting and understanding the influences of celestial bodies on our lives. In this section, we will dive into the depths of astrological houses, exploring their significance and how they shape our destiny.

Astrological houses represent different areas of our lives, essentially acting as the stage upon which the planets perform their cosmic dance. Each house represents a distinct aspect, from personal identity and relationships to career and spirituality. Understanding the meaning and significance of each house is vital for any high magic student seeking to master the art of astrology.

The twelve astrological houses are divided across the zodiac wheel, with each house occupying a specific segment. The first house, also known as the Ascendant, represents our identity and how we present ourselves to the world. It is the foundation upon which our entire astrological chart is built. As we move clockwise around the wheel, each subsequent house unfolds a different aspect of our lives, such as finances, communication, and home life.

Tarot card readers and interpreters can benefit greatly from understanding astrological houses. By incorporating the knowledge of houses into their readings, they can provide deeper insights into a client's life journey. For example, if the seeker draws cards representing love and relationships in the seventh house, it suggests that partnership and marriage will play a significant role in their life path.

Astrologers and horoscope analysts rely heavily on astrological houses to provide accurate and insightful predictions. By observing the planets' positions within these houses, they can decipher the potential influences on an individual's life. For instance, if Mars is positioned in the tenth house, it indicates a strong drive for career success and ambition.

Divination techniques, such as scrying and pendulum dowsing, can also be enhanced through an understanding of astrological houses. These practices, which involve tapping into the cosmic energies, can be further refined by aligning them with the corresponding house's theme. Scrying with a focus on the eighth house, which represents transformation and the high, may yield profound insights into one's spiritual journey.

In conclusion, astrological houses are crucial components of astrology, providing a framework for understanding the influences of celestial bodies on our lives. Whether you are a tarot card reader, astrologer, or divination practitioner, delving into the depths of astrological houses will unlock a wealth of knowledge and insight. By comprehending the unique significance of each house, you will navigate the intricate tapestry of the cosmos, empowering yourself to offer guidance and enlightenment to those seeking answers.

The First House

The First House, often referred to as the house of self, governs our identity, appearance, and overall outlook on life. As the first and most important house in the astrological chart, it sets the stage for the entire horoscope analysis, providing valuable insights into our personality, temperament, and physical attributes.

In tarot card reading and interpretation, the First House corresponds to the Fool, the card of new beginnings and unlimited potential. This alignment signifies the adventurous spirit and openness to new experiences that are characteristic of individuals strongly influenced by the First House. By understanding the energy of this house, tarot readers can gain a deeper understanding of their clients' personalities and life paths.

For those practicing astrology, the First House serves as the foundation upon which the entire birth chart is built. It represents the "mask" we wear, reflecting how we present ourselves to the world. By examining the planet(s) and zodiac sign(s) residing in the First House, astrologers can uncover valuable clues about an individual's character, motivations, and even physical appearance.

Moreover, divination techniques and practices, such as scrying and pendulum dowsing, can also benefit from an understanding of the First House. By incorporating the energy of this house into their sessions, practitioners can gain deeper insights into the questions posed by their clients. Whether scrying into a crystal ball or using a pendulum to communicate with the divine, tapping into the power of the First House enhances the accuracy and depth of the readings.

Understanding the wisdom of the First House and its influence allows you to develop a greater awareness of yourself and others, enabling you to provide more insightful and meaningful interpretations. So, dear high magic students, dive deep into the mysteries of the First House and unlock the secrets that lie within. May your path be illuminated by the knowledge you gain, and may your divination skills soar to new heights!

The Second House

The Second House, traditionally associated with material possessions, financial stability, and personal values, plays a pivotal role in understanding an individual's relationship with wealth and abundance. In astrology, this house represents the tangible assets and resources one acquires throughout their life. By studying the Second House in a birth chart, you can gain profound insights into a person's financial prospects, spending habits, and overall sense of worth.

Tarot card reading and interpretation can be significantly enhanced by incorporating the knowledge of the Second House. By understanding the correlation between specific cards and financial matters, you will be able to provide more accurate and comprehensive readings for your clients. For instance, the appearance of the Five of Pentacles may suggest financial struggles or a need for careful budgeting, while the Ten of Pentacles indicates a period of stability and prosperity.

The Second House is not limited to financial matters alone. It also offers insights into an individual's personal values and self-worth. By exploring this aspect, you can guide your clients towards a deeper understanding of their intrinsic worth and help them align their actions with their core beliefs.

In addition to tarot card reading and astrology, the Second House also finds relevance in various divination techniques and practices, such as scrying and pendulum dowsing. By using these methods, you can tap into the energy of the Second House and gain even more profound insights into your own life or the lives of your clients.

Remember that the Second House is not an isolated entity, but rather interconnected with the entire birth chart. By studying this house with other astrological aspects, you will be able to provide a more comprehensive analysis and guide your clients towards a more fulfilling and abundant life.

In conclusion, the Second House holds immense potential for high magic students, particularly those specializing in tarot card reading, astrology, and various divination techniques. By understanding the significance of this house in relation to finances, personal values, and self-worth, you will be able to provide more accurate readings and guidance to your clients. So, dive into the enchanting world of the Second House and unlock the secrets it holds for you and those seeking your divination skills.

The Third House

The Third House is a celestial abode that unveils hidden truths about communication, intellect, and the power of the spoken word. As manifestation or magik students, delving into the secrets of the Third House will allow you to enhance your understanding of Tarot card reading and interpretation, astrology and horoscope analysis, as well as various divination techniques and practices such as scrying and pendulum dowsing.

The Third House, traditionally associated with the zodiac sign Gemini, is often referred to as the House of Communication. It governs all forms of expression, written or verbal, and encompasses the art of interpretation. Within this cosmic dwelling, the energy of Mercury, the messenger of the gods, reigns supreme. As you explore the Third House, you will learn to harness this celestial force to unlock the mysteries of divination.

Tarot card reading and interpretation are deeply enriched by the knowledge of the Third House. By understanding the astrological correspondences and symbolism associated with each card, you will gain a deeper insight into the messages they convey. As you grasp the essence of communication, you will unlock the wisdom hidden within the Tarot's archetypal imagery, allowing you to provide more accurate and profound readings for yourself and others.

Astrology and horoscope analysis also find their roots in the Third House. By studying the positioning of Mercury in the natal chart, you will gain insights into an individual's communication style, intellectual pursuits, and mental agility. This knowledge will enable you to decipher the hidden potentials and challenges that lie within their celestial blueprint, guiding you to provide more comprehensive and personalized horoscope interpretations.

Moreover, the Third House is a gateway to various divination techniques and practices. Through scrying, the art of gazing into reflective surfaces or crystal balls, you can tap into your intuitive powers and unlock hidden truths. Pendulum dowsing, on the other hand, allows you to communicate with your higher self and receive guidance from the cosmos. By aligning these practices with the energies of the Third House, you will enhance your ability to access the realms beyond the physical and unveil the answers you seek.

As you embark on your journey through the Third

House, the realm of communication, intellect, and divination will begin to unveil its secrets. By integrating this knowledge into your studies of Tarot card reading and interpretation, astrology and horoscope analysis, as well as divination techniques and practices, you will become a truly skilled high magic student, capable of navigating the intricate tapestry of the metaphysical world.

Embrace the wisdom of the Third House, and let it guide you on your path of divination mastery.

The Fourth House

Known as the house of home, family, and roots, it holds the key to understanding the foundations upon which our lives are built.

As you explore the Fourth House, you will discover how it influences our emotional wellbeing, childhood experiences, and the dynamics within our family. This house provides valuable insights into our ancestral heritage and the psychological patterns that shape our existence. By understanding the Fourth House, you will gain a deeper understanding of your past, present, and future.

Tarot card reading and interpretation aficionados, pay attention! The Fourth House is closely associated with the Major Arcana card, "The Chariot." In this section, we will explore the connections between this card and the Fourth House, unraveling the symbolism and meaning behind it. This knowledge will enhance your tarot readings and enable you to provide more profound insights to your clients.

Moreover, divination techniques and practices such as scrying and pendulum dowsing can be enriched by incorporating the Fourth House into your readings. By understanding the energies associated with this house, you will gain a deeper understanding of the information revealed through these divination methods. Whether you are scrying into a reflective surface or using a pendulum to communicate with the spiritual realm, the Fourth House will provide you with a broader perspective.

As we conclude our exploration of the Fourth House, remember that this knowledge is a powerful tool in your divination arsenal. The insights gained from understanding the Fourth House will enable you to provide more accurate and comprehensive readings.

Embrace the wisdom of the celestial bodies and let the Fourth House guide you on your journey of self-discovery and divination mastery.

Continue your studies, my friends, and let the Fourth House unveil the secrets that lie within. May your tarot readings, astrology analyses, and divination practices be elevated to new heights as you incorporate the wisdom of the Fourth House into your craft.

The Fifth House

In the realm of divination, there exists a mystical house that holds immense power and significance - the Fifth House. As divination students, you are about to embark on a journey into the depths of ancient divination techniques, and it is within the Fifth House that we uncover the secrets of the cosmos and the profound connection between the celestial and earthly realms.

Tarot card reading and interpretation, astrology and horoscope analysis, and various divination practices such as scrying and pendulum dowsing all find their essence illuminated within the Fifth House. This chapter will serve as your guide to understanding the immense potential and wisdom that lies within this enigmatic realm.

The Fifth House, often referred to as the House of Creativity and Pleasure, is ruled by the Sun and governs matters of self-expression, love, romance, and personal fulfillment. Within the realm of tarot card reading and interpretation, it is here that we uncover the true significance of the cards related to creativity, passion, and matters of the heart. Through the exploration of archetypes and symbolism within tarot, we gain insight into the depths of human emotions and desires.

Astrology enthusiasts will find solace within the Fifth House, as it governs matters related to love affairs, children, and artistic endeavors. By analyzing the placement of planets such as Venus and the Moon within this house, we unlock the secrets of our romantic inclinations, creative potentials, and even the potential for fertility and childbirth.

Divination techniques such as scrying and pendulum dowsing also find their resonance within the Fifth House. By tapping into the intuitive abilities that lie dormant within each of us, we can harness the power of these practices to gain valuable insight into matters of the heart, creative endeavors, and personal fulfillment.

As high magic students, it is crucial to recognize the profound connection between the celestial and earthly realms that the Fifth House embodies. By delving into the wisdom and energy of this house, we unlock the door to profound self-discovery and the ability to navigate the complexities of love, creativity, and personal fulfillment.

Next, we will explore the intricacies of tarot card reading and interpretation within the Fifth House, delve into the depths of astrology and horoscope analysis, and uncover the ancient divination techniques that have been used for centuries to unlock the secrets of the universe. Prepare yourselves, high magic students, for a journey that will forever transform the way you perceive and interact with the world around you. The Fifth House awaits, ready to bestow its ancient wisdom upon those who dare to seek it.

The Sixth House

The Sixth House, also known as the House of Health, is a significant aspect of astrology. It holds valuable insights into matters of physical well-being, daily routines, work, and service. By understanding the influence of this house, you can gain a deeper understanding of yourself and others.

In the realm of Tarot card reading and interpretation, the Sixth House can be associated with the suit of Pentacles, which symbolizes the material aspects of life. When a Pentacle card appears in a reading, it may indicate a need for attention to one's health, work-life balance, or the importance of practicality. As an high magic student, incorporating the Sixth House into your Tarot readings will enhance your interpretations and provide valuable guidance to your clients.

Astrology enthusiasts will find the Sixth House particularly intriguing. By analyzing the placement of planets within this house in a birth chart, astrologers can gain insight into an individual's attitude towards work, health issues that may arise, and the potential for a fulfilling career. Furthermore, the interplay of other houses with the Sixth House can reveal intricate details about one's daily routines, habits, and even pet ownership.

For those interested in divination techniques and

practices, the Sixth House offers an avenue for exploration. Consider incorporating scrying or pendulum dowsing to gain insights into your physical well-being or work-related matters. By focusing your intent on the Sixth House, you may unlock hidden knowledge and receive guidance on health concerns or ways to improve your productivity and overall satisfaction in life.

In summary, the Sixth House is a crucial aspect of astrology with significant implications for Tarot card reading, astrology and horoscope analysis, as well as divination techniques and practices. high magic students specializing in these niches will greatly benefit from exploring the intricacies of this house. By understanding the influence of the Sixth House, you can enhance your divination skills and provide valuable insights to those seeking guidance in matters of health, work, and daily routines.

The Seventh House

The Seventh House, also known as the House of Relationships, is a celestial gateway that unveils the intricate tapestry of connections between individuals, both romantic and platonic. As the sun sets on the horizon, this house rises, bringing forth the delicate dance of partnerships, alliances, and the pursuit of harmony in our lives.

Tarot enthusiasts will find themselves drawn into the

realm of the Seventh House as they explore the intricate meanings behind the cards that reside within. The cards in this house speak of love, commitment, and the various dynamics that shape our relationships. Delve into the symbolism and interpretation of cards like The Lovers, Two of Cups, and The Hierophant, and unlock the secrets of the Seventh House through your Tarot deck.

Astrology aficionados will discover that the Seventh House serves as a celestial mirror, reflecting the influence of the planets on our connections with others. Dive deep into the birth chart and uncover how the Seventh House reveals the nature of your partnerships and the potential challenges you may encounter on your journey. Discover the significance of Venus, Mars, and Jupiter as they move through this house, shaping the ebb and flow of your relationships.

For those seeking to expand their divination toolkit, the Seventh House offers a gateway to the world of scrying and pendulum dowsing. Peer into the reflective surfaces and let your intuition guide you as you uncover hidden truths about your relationships. Or harness the power of the pendulum as it swings and sways, providing answers to your most burning questions about love and connection.

Whether you are a seasoned practitioner or a curious novice, the Seventh House holds the key to unraveling the intricate web of relationships that shape our lives. Open your mind and embark on a journey that will deepen your understanding of Tarot card reading, astrology, and various divination techniques. Expand your repertoire, refine your skills, and embrace the mysteries of the Seventh House as you navigate the realm of high magic.

The Eighth House

The Eighth House is often considered one of the most enigmatic and intense areas of the astrological chart. It is associated with deep transformation, shared resources, and the mysteries of life and death. As tarot card readers, understanding the Eighth House can enhance your interpretations, especially when exploring themes of endings, rebirth, and hidden influences. The House's connection to the Death card, for instance, can offer profound insights into the transformative energies at play.

Astrology and horoscope analysis enthusiasts will find the Eighth House a treasure trove of hidden meanings and profound revelations. It governs matters such as inheritance, joint finances, and metaphysical experiences. By analyzing the planets and signs present in this House, astrologers can uncover the individual's approach to intimacy, metaphysical abilities, and even their attitude towards shared resources.

For those interested in divination techniques and practices, the Eighth House holds significant importance. Ancient divination methods like scrying, where one gazes into a reflective surface to gain insights, can be greatly enhanced when performed in the presence of eighth house energies. The House's associations with the subconscious mind and hidden truths make it an ideal setting for pendulum dowsing, a technique used to access the depths of the psyche and receive guidance from the unseen realms.

As high magic students, it is crucial to embrace the profound power of the Eighth House in our divination practices. By exploring the symbolism, planetary influences, and astrological aspects connected to this House, we can unlock its transformative potential. The Eighth House invites us to confront our fears, explore the depths of our psyche, and tap into hidden resources that can aid us in our spiritual journey.

In conclusion, the Eighth House is a realm of mystery, transformation, and hidden treasures. Whether you are a tarot card reader, astrology enthusiast, or divination practitioner, understanding this House's significance can enrich your readings, interpretations, and divination practices. Embrace the profound energies of the Eighth House, and let it guide you towards the depths of the high and the wonders of ancient divination techniques.

The Ninth House

The Ninth House is a significant aspect of astrology and horoscope analysis as it represents several important aspects such as expansion, higher learning, and spiritual growth. The association of this activity is with exploring foreign cultures, searching for higher truths, and undertaking long-distance travel. The Ninth House plays a crucial role for those who aspire to be astrologers, as it guides us towards expanding our perspectives, delving deeper into our knowledge, and exploring the very depths of our existence. The domain we are referring to is the vast expanse of the universe, where we can observe celestial bodies and planets that have a significant impact on our search for knowledge and understanding.

The Ninth House is a vital piece of the puzzle for those seeking to understand the intricacies of tarot card reading and interpretation, as it holds important clues that can help unravel the mysteries of the cards. If you happen to come across a spread featuring this house, it indicates that you have a desire for exploration, self-discovery, and knowledge. It prompts us to seek new experiences and embark on journeys of the mind, body, and soul. The Ninth House urges tarot readers to encourage their querents to embrace their curiosity and venture beyond their comfort zones.

The Ninth House is a gateway to exploring the higher realms of consciousness through divination techniques such as scrying, pendulum dowsing, and other practices. To access the hidden wisdom and receive divine guidance from these ancient arts, practitioners must tap into the energy of the Ninth House. By means of scrying, individuals can gaze into reflective surfaces, such as mirrors or crystal balls, in order to gain insight and discover truths that will help them along their spiritual journey. Pendulum dowsing, on the other hand, allows diviners to communicate with the subconscious mind and the higher self, unveiling answers to questions that dwell within.

Understanding the significance of the Ninth House and showing it respect is an essential part of being a high magic student. Take advantage of the vast energy that is available and allow it to guide you towards a deep transformation and spiritual enlightenment. Immerse yourself in the rich teachings of astrology, tarot, and other forms of divination, as the Ninth House expertly guides you through your journey towards becoming an intuitive and skilled diviner.

Remember, the Ninth House represents the gateway to wisdom, growth, and exploration. Embrace its influence, and let it propel you towards unlocking the ancient secrets that lie within the depths of your divinatory practices.

The Tenth House

Astrology enthusiasts and tarot card readers alike understand the importance of the Tenth House, also known as the Midheaven, as it holds the key to one's career, reputation, and public image. This celestial house represents our ambitions, goals, and the pinnacle of success we strive to achieve in our lives.

The Tenth House is an important aspect to consider when examining a birth chart as it sheds light on the individual's vocational path, offering insights into the skills and talents that can potentially propel them to great heights in their chosen career. The insights that it provides are crucial in determining an individual's potential for leadership, authority, and recognition in the field they have chosen. For individuals who are looking for guidance in their professional endeavors, comprehending the energy of this house is of utmost importance.

For tarot card readers, the Tenth House corresponds with certain Major Arcana cards, such as The Emperor or The World. These cards symbolize power, authority, and worldly achievements. Exploring the Tenth House in conjunction with tarot card interpretation can enhance your readings by providing a deeper understanding of an individual's career prospects and the influences that shape their professional life.

Moreover, the exploration of various divination techniques and practices associated with the Tenth House is also covered in this section. For instance, scrying, a method of gazing into reflective surfaces or crystal balls to gain insight, can be used to tap into the energies of this celestial house. Pendulum dowsing, another powerful divination tool, can help high magic students connect with the vibrations of the Tenth House, providing answers and guidance regarding career choices and life purpose.

By studying the Tenth House, astrologers, tarot card readers, and divination enthusiasts can empower themselves and their clients by unraveling the mysteries of professional success and reputation. Whether you are seeking personal guidance or aiming to enhance your divination practice, the knowledge contained within this section will prove invaluable.

The Tenth House is also associated with the zodiac sign of Capricorn, which is known for its ambition, determination, and hardworking nature. These qualities are reflected in the energy of the Tenth House, which encourages individuals to strive for success and recognition in their chosen field.

However, it is important to note that the Tenth House is not just about material success and worldly achievements. It also encompasses one's reputation and public image, which can be affected by their actions and behavior in both their personal and professional lives.

Astrologers often look at the planetary placements in the Tenth House to gain a deeper understanding of an individual's career prospects and potential obstacles. For instance, the presence of Saturn in the Tenth House may indicate challenges and setbacks in one's career, while the placement of Jupiter can signify abundance and success.

Tarot card readers, on the other hand, may use the Tenth House as a reference point to interpret the cards in a spread. For instance, if the Emperor card appears in the career position of a tarot spread, it may suggest that the individual is in a position of authority or leadership in their profession.

Overall, the Tenth House holds great significance in astrology, tarot card reading, and divination practices. By understanding its energy and symbolism, individuals can gain valuable insights into their career path, reputation, and potential for success.

Take the opportunity to immerse yourself in the secrets of the Tenth House, where you can unlock the hidden potential of astrology, tarot card reading, and divination techniques. If you are willing to embrace the wisdom of the ancients, you can start a journey that will lead to self-discovery, career fulfillment, and spiritual growth.

The Eleventh House

Unlocking the Secrets of Social Connections

The eleventh house in astrology is associated with various aspects of one's social life, friendships, hopes, dreams, and aspirations. The eleventh house is often referred to as the "House of Friends" or "House of Hopes and Wishes."

In this house, one's social circle is highlighted, including their relationships with peers, colleagues, and acquaintances. The eleventh house also governs one's involvement in group activities, such as clubs, organizations, and social gatherings. This house is also linked to one's hopes, dreams, and aspirations, as it represents the future and the potential for growth and success. The eleventh house is ruled by Aquarius, and those with strong placements in this house are often known for their innovative and unconventional ideas. Overall, the eleventh house in astrology plays a crucial role in shaping one's social identity and future prospects.

Tarot Card Reading and Interpretation:

Within the Eleventh House, tarot card enthusiasts will find a treasure trove of insights into friendships, alliances, and the impact of group dynamics on an individual's life path. As you explore the Eleventh House, you will discover the hidden messages within the cards that foretell how your social connections will shape your destiny. Uncover the true power of the Tarot in illuminating the intricate web of relationships that surround us.

Astrology and Horoscope Analysis:

If you happen to be interested in astrology, then you might find it interesting to know that the Eleventh House can provide a celestial gateway through which you can gain an understanding of the significance of friendships, groups, and associations in your astrological chart.

By exploring the cosmic energies that affect your social interactions, you can gain insight into how the placement of planets in your house can impact your capacity to establish and sustain significant relationships. By exploring the Eleventh House, which serves as a celestial compass, you will be able to navigate towards relationships that are harmonious and fulfilling.

Divination Techniques and Practices:

In the realm of divination techniques and practices, the Eleventh House holds profound secrets waiting to be unveiled. Whether you are a practitioner of scrying, pendulum dowsing, or other forms of divination, this house provides a lens through which you can gain deeper insights into the social fabric of your life. Peer into the depths of the Eleventh House to discover the hidden patterns that shape your interactions with others, allowing you to navigate the intricate tapestry of human connections with wisdom and foresight.

As you embark on this mystical journey through the Eleventh House, remember that true enlightenment lies not only in the knowledge you acquire but also in the application of that knowledge. Embrace the wisdom of the ancients, and let the Eleventh House empower you to create meaningful relationships, forge alliances, and unlock the secrets of your own social destiny.

May the divination techniques and practices you encounter within the Eleventh House guide you towards greater self-awareness, deeper connections, and a profound understanding of the intricate dance between individual and collective destinies. Open your minds, fellow seekers, and embrace the magic that awaits you within the Eleventh House.

The Twelfth House

The enigmatic Twelfth House – a realm shrouded in

mystery and intrigue within the realm of high magic. As high magic students, you are already well-versed in various divination techniques, such as tarot card reading, astrology, and the practice of divination techniques like scrying and pendulum dowsing. In this section, we will delve deeper into the secrets held by the Twelfth House, uncovering the hidden wisdom it offers.

In astrology, the Twelfth House is often associated with hidden realms, secrets, and the unconscious mind. It is known as the house of self-undoing, spirituality, dreams, and the hidden aspects of our psyche.

The Twelfth House is a complex and multifaceted realm of high magic that requires patience and persistence to understand fully. However, the rewards of delving deep into this mysterious realm are immense. By exploring the Twelfth House, you can gain a deeper understanding of your spiritual path and develop a stronger connection to your intuition.

One of the most important things to remember when working with the Twelfth House is to approach it with an open mind and heart. This house is not about finding easy answers or quick solutions. Instead, it is about exploring the hidden aspects of your psyche, facing your fears, and embracing the unknown.

To begin your exploration of the Twelfth House,

start by learning more about the symbolism associated with this realm. The Moon, for example, is a card that often appears in readings related to the Twelfth House. This card represents the hidden aspects of the self, including fears, secrets, and desires. By studying the symbolism of the Moon and other cards related to the Twelfth House, you can gain a deeper understanding of the messages contained within your readings.

In addition to tarot card reading, astrology and horoscope analysis can also provide valuable insights into the Twelfth House. Pay close attention to the placement of planets in this house, as this can reveal important information about your spiritual journey and the hidden aspects of your personality.

Finally, don't forget about the power of divination techniques like scrying and pendulum dowsing. By tapping into the energy of the Twelfth House, you can access the hidden realms and receive powerful messages from the divine.

In conclusion, the Twelfth House is a rich and complex realm of high magic that holds many secrets and hidden wisdom. By exploring this realm, you can gain a deeper understanding of yourself and others and develop your divination skills to new heights. So embrace the mysteries of the Twelfth House and let its magic guide you on your spiritual journey.

Chapter Eleven

Analyzing Birth Charts and Horoscopes

Astrology and horoscope analysis have long been revered for their ability to provide a roadmap of our lives, revealing our strengths, weaknesses, and potential challenges. By studying the positions and movements of celestial bodies at the time of our birth, we can gain valuable insights into our personalities, relationships, and life paths.

In this chapter, we will explore the fundamentals of birth chart analysis. We will learn how to decipher the unique symbolism of each planet, house, and aspect within a birth chart and understand how they intertwine to shape our lives. We will also delve into the significance of the rising sign, sun sign, and moon sign, unraveling their influence on our identities and emotional landscapes.

To truly grasp the intricacies of birth chart

interpretation, we will delve into the art of synthesizing information. By studying the interplay between planetary aspects and the houses they inhabit, we can uncover hidden patterns and unveil the deeper meanings behind our experiences. We will discover how to identify dominant planetary energies and understand their impact on our lives.

Furthermore, we will explore the connection between birth charts and horoscopes, learning how to create accurate and insightful horoscope readings for ourselves and others.

We will unravel the significance of planetary transits, progressions, and retrogrades, gaining the ability to predict and navigate the ebbs and flows of our lives.

As high magic students, this section will provide you with the tools and knowledge needed to unlock the secrets of birth charts and horoscopes. By mastering this ancient divination technique, you will be able to offer profound insights and guidance to yourself and those seeking your expertise.

Whether you are drawn to Tarot card reading and interpretation, astrology, or various divination techniques such as scrying or pendulum dowsing, the art of analyzing birth charts and horoscopes will deepen your understanding of the mystical forces that shape our lives. Get ready to embark on a transformative journey and unlock the celestial wisdom that lies within the stars.

The Sun Sign

Among the various aspects of astrology, the Sun Sign, also known as the zodiac sign, is a fundamental element that plays a crucial role in understanding an individual's personality, destiny, and life path.

The Sun Sign represents the position of the Sun at the time of your birth and is determined by the date you were born. It is believed to embody the essence of your true self, illuminating your core strengths, weaknesses, and unique characteristics. By exploring and interpreting your Sun Sign, you can gain valuable insights into your personality traits, relationships, and life purpose.

Tarot card reading and interpretation, a popular divination practice, can be enhanced by understanding the Sun Sign. By incorporating the knowledge of the Sun Sign into your readings, you can provide your clients with a deeper understanding of their personalities and life journeys. For instance, a Leo with their powerful and charismatic nature may be drawn to cards representing leadership and creativity, while a Cancer with their nurturing and intuitive tendencies may resonate with cards symbolizing emotions and family.

Astrology and horoscope analysis, another niche

within the high arts, heavily rely on the Sun Sign. By examining the alignment of the planets and their relationship to the Sun at the time of an individual's birth, astrologers can unveil the cosmic blueprint of their life.

Understanding the Sun Sign allows astrologers to provide accurate and insightful horoscope readings, highlighting the potential challenges and opportunities that lie ahead.

Furthermore, the knowledge of the Sun Sign is not limited to astrology and tarot alone, but extends to various divination techniques and practices. Whether you are engaging in scrying, pendulum dowsing, or any other form of divination, the Sun Sign can offer guidance and clarity in uncovering hidden truths and deeper meanings.

As high magic students, embracing the wisdom of the Sun Sign opens up a vast realm of possibilities for exploration and self- discovery. By delving into the unique characteristics and influences of each zodiac sign, you will embark on a journey of unraveling the mysteries of the universe and unlocking the secrets of your own destiny.

Remember, the Sun Sign is but one piece of the intricate puzzle that is your existence. It serves as a guiding light, leading you towards a deeper understanding of yourself and the world around you. So, let the Sun Sign be your compass as you navigate the vast and enchanting realm of divination and high practices.

The Moon Sign

While most are familiar with the influence of the sun and the zodiac signs, the moon often remains an enigma. However, for those delving into the depths of high magic, knowledge of the moon sign is essential for unlocking the secrets of the universe.

Tarot card reading and interpretation, astrology and horoscope analysis, and divination techniques and practices all converge under the guidance of the moon sign. As high magic students, you are no doubt aware of the power that the moon holds and its ability to shape our lives and destinies. In this section, we shall explore the profound impact of the moon sign and how it can be utilized to enhance your divination skills.

The moon sign represents our emotional nature, instincts, and subconscious mind. It reveals our hidden desires, dreams, and how we process emotions. Just as the moon waxes and wanes, our emotions fluctuate in a similar manner. By understanding the moon sign, we can gain profound insights into our own emotional landscape and that of others, enabling us to provide more accurate and meaningful interpretations.

For tarot card readers, incorporating the moon sign

into your readings can unlock a deeper understanding of the cards. The moon sign provides a nuanced perspective, shedding light on the emotional undercurrents that influence the querent's situation. By considering both the zodiac sign and the moon sign, you can elevate your interpretations to a new level of insight and clarity.

Astrologers and horoscope analysts can utilize the moon sign to provide a comprehensive understanding of an individual's personality and life path. By examining the moon's placement at the time of birth, astrologers can decipher how the individual processes and expresses their emotions. This knowledge allows for more accurate predictions and guidance regarding relationships, career choices, and personal growth.

Additionally, divination techniques and practices such as scrying and pendulum dowsing can be enhanced by incorporating the moon sign. The moon's energy acts as a conduit, amplifying our intuitive abilities and providing a deeper connection to the spiritual realm. By aligning your divination practices with the moon sign, you can tap into a wellspring of wisdom and insight that might otherwise remain hidden.

In conclusion, the moon sign holds immense power within the realm of high magic. By understanding its influence and incorporating it into tarot card readings, astrology and horoscope analysis, and divination techniques, you can elevate your skills to new heights.

Embrace the moon's guidance and allow it to illuminate the path to deeper understanding and enlightenment.

The Ascendant Sign

One cannot underestimate the power and influence of the Ascendant Sign. Known as the rising sign, it is a crucial component in understanding an individual's personality and destiny. This section aims to shed light on this celestial phenomenon, providing high magic students with essential knowledge to enhance their tarot card reading and interpretation, astrology and horoscope analysis, as well as divination techniques and practices.

The Ascendant Sign is determined by the zodiac constellation that was rising on the eastern horizon at the exact moment of an individual's birth. It acts as a filter for the person's energy, molding their outward appearance, behavior, and overall approach to life. It is the mask we wear, the first impression we make, and the lens through which we see the world.

In the realm of tarot card reading and interpretation, understanding the Ascendant Sign can bring a new level of depth to your readings. By incorporating the traits and characteristics associated with the Ascendant Sign, you can provide more accurate and personalized insights to your clients. For example, a Leo Ascendant may indicate a natural flair for creativity and leadership, while a Scorpio Ascendant could suggest a deep, intuitive nature.

Astrology and horoscope analysis also benefit from a thorough understanding of the Ascendant Sign. It provides a vital piece of information in constructing an individual's natal chart, enabling astrologers to accurately interpret the positioning of the planets and their influence on various aspects of life. The Ascendant Sign offers a unique perspective on an individual's personality, relationships, career, and overall life path.

Divination techniques and practices such as scrying and pendulum dowsing can be enhanced by incorporating the Ascendant Sign. By attuning yourself to the energy associated with the rising sign, you can tap into a deeper level of intuition and connection with the spiritual realm. This opens up new avenues for divination and allows for more accurate and insightful readings.

In conclusion, the Ascendant Sign is an invaluable tool for high magic students, particularly those interested in tarot card reading and interpretation, astrology and horoscope analysis, as well as various divination techniques and practices. By delving into the depths of this celestial phenomenon, you can unlock a wealth of knowledge and understanding, enabling you to provide more accurate and personalized readings for yourself and your clients. Embrace the power of the Ascendant Sign and watch as your divination skills soar to new heights.

The Planetary Aspects

In order to unlock the mysteries of the cosmos, it is crucial to have an understanding of the planetary aspects, which play a significant role. You, as high magic students, have already acquired a wealth of knowledge and experience in different divination practices, such as tarot card reading, astrology and horoscope analysis, scrying, and pendulum dowsing, to name a few. Although the subject may seem daunting at first, taking the time to explore the planetary aspects will undoubtedly provide you with a deeper understanding of the celestial forces that shape and influence our lives.

The planets, with their unique energies and symbolism, play a vital role in divination. Each planet represents specific qualities and attributes, and when they interact with one another in the sky, they form what is known as planetary aspects. These aspects create a dynamic dance of energy that can greatly influence our interpretations and predictions.

When studying tarot card reading and interpretation, incorporating the planetary aspects can enhance your understanding of the cards. For instance, recognizing the influence of Mercury, the planet of communication and intellect, can shed light on the meaning of cards related to communication and mental processes.

Similarly, the presence of Venus, the planet of love and beauty, may indicate themes of romance or artistic expression.

Astrology and horoscope analysis also benefit greatly from an understanding of the planetary aspects. The aspects formed by the planets at the time of birth or during significant events can reveal important insights into an individual's personality, relationships, and life path. For instance, a challenging aspect between Mars and Saturn may indicate obstacles and lessons to be learned, while a harmonious aspect between Venus and Jupiter may signify good fortune and abundance.

Moreover, in divination techniques like scrying and pendulum dowsing, incorporating the planetary aspects can deepen your connection to the unseen realms. By aligning your practice with the current planetary positions, you can tap into the specific energies and vibrations associated with each planet. This alignment not only enhances your ability to receive messages, but also provides a framework for interpretation.

In conclusion, the planetary aspects are a valuable tool for high magic students, particularly those interested in tarot card reading and interpretation, astrology and horoscope analysis, and various divination techniques. By incorporating the planetary energies into your practice, you will unlock a deeper level of insight and understanding. Remember, the planets are not merely celestial bodies; they are the keys that unlock the secrets of the universe. Embrace the planetary aspects, and let the cosmic dance guide your divination journey.

The Houses in the Birth Chart

(Gee, didn't we already go over this? Yeah, but....) (I'll try to be brief.)

The birth chart serves as a road-map to understanding the unique energies and influences that shape an individual's life. At the heart of this intricate cosmic map lie the Houses - twelve divisions that represent specific areas of life and the various aspects they govern. To grasp the true essence of astrology, high magic students, particularly those with a keen interest in tarot card reading and interpretation, astrology and horoscope analysis, as well as divination techniques and practices, must delve into the profound significance of these Houses.

Each House in the birth chart represents a distinct facet of human existence, offering valuable insights into different realms of experience. From the moment we take our first breath, the planets align within these Houses, casting their divine influence upon our lives. Understanding the Houses empowers us to navigate the ebbs and flows of life's intricate tapestry with greater clarity and comprehension.

The First House, also known as the Ascendant, holds the key to our identity and how we present ourselves to the world. It signifies our physical appearance, demeanor, and overall personality. The Second House delves into matters of personal wealth, possessions, and material resources, probing the depths of our financial well-being and values.

Moving forward, the Third House governs communication, siblings, and short journeys, unraveling the threads of our immediate environment and relationships with relatives. The Fourth House, also known as the House of Home, pertains to our roots, family, and the nurturing aspects of our lives.

Venturing into the Fifth House, we encounter the realm of creativity, romance, and children. It unravels our passions, artistic inclinations, and the joys derived from love and self- expression. The Sixth House, on the other hand, delves into health, work, and daily routines, examining our physical well-being and the nature of our jobs.

As we progress to the Seventh House, the focus shifts to partnerships, marriage, and relationships. This House explores our capacity for cooperation, harmony, and the dynamics of our one-on-one connections. The Eighth House delves into deeper, transformative experiences, including shared resources, sexuality, and spiritual growth.

The Ninth House expands our horizons, encompassing higher education, philosophy, and long-distance travel. It pushes the boundaries of our intellectual and spiritual pursuits. The Tenth House, often associated with career and public image, uncovers our aspirations, achievements, and societal standing.

Moving towards completion, the Eleventh House represents friendships, social networks, and our involvement within communities. It sheds light on our hopes, dreams, and our capacity to connect with like-minded individuals. Finally, the Twelfth House, the realm of the subconscious mind, spirituality, and hidden forces, unravels the mysteries that lie beneath the surface of our conscious existence.

Understanding the Houses in the birth chart is essential for those fascinated with tarot card reading and interpretation, astrology and horoscope analysis, as well as divination techniques and practices. By deciphering the influence of each House, practitioners gain a profound understanding of the intricate interplay between celestial energies and human experience, empowering them to unlock the secrets of the cosmos and guide others through their spiritual journeys with wisdom and insight.

Chapter Twelve

Other Divination Methods

Scrying: Gazing into the Future

One ancient divination technique that continues to captivate the minds of seekers is scrying. You see it all the time in cartoons. A mysterious setting, a fortune teller gazing into a crystal ball. A scene with a wizard and crystal ball was pivotal in Wizard of Oz.

Scrying, often referred to as "gazing," is a practice that allows the diviner to tap into their inner visions and receive messages from the spiritual realm. Throughout history, scrying has been used by mystics, seers, and witches to gain insight into the past, present, and future. By using various mediums, such as a crystal ball, a mirror, or a bowl of water, the diviner can enter a state of deep concentration and clarity to access hidden knowledge.

Scrying is a technique where one gazes at a device and begins to pull psychic information. Whether it's the reflective surface of a mirror or the ethereal depths of a crystal ball, each medium has its own energy and symbolism, which can enhance the diviner's connection to the unseen. We will also discuss ways to cleanse and charge these tools, ensuring they are attuned to your own personal energy.

Next, we delve into the techniques and practices of scrying. We will guide you through the process of entering a meditative state, quieting the mind, and opening yourself to receive intuitive messages. Through step-by- step instructions, you will learn how to focus your gaze and interpret the symbols and images that arise. We will also explore the significance of different colors, shapes, and patterns that may appear during a scrying session.

Furthermore, we will touch upon the ethics and responsibilities of scrying. While gazing into the future can be exciting and enlightening, it is crucial to approach this practice with respect and integrity. We will discuss the importance of consent, personal boundaries, and ethical considerations when sharing the information received through scrying.

Whether you are a seasoned practitioner or new to

the world of divination, scrying offers a powerful tool for expanding your intuitive abilities and exploring the unknown. By incorporating scrying into your repertoire, you will gain a deeper understanding of the interconnectedness of the past, present, and future.

Open your mind, sharpen your gaze, and let the secrets of the future reveal themselves to you.

Crystal Ball Scrying

Crystal ball. I mean, this is THE symbol of Fortune Telling. I've lost count how many cartoons I see where someone is getting their future "read" by someone with a crystal ball.

And, I can't make them work.

My first attempt was a few weeks after buying a crystal ball for a prop in a photo shoot. I figured, hey - why not? Ya know? So, I went online with a search engine called "Alta Vista" and looked up the instructions.

I gave it a shot. I used a dark room; I meditated. I'd peer into the depths of the crystal ball.

And nothing. Zip. Zero.

So, I kept trying.

My daughter, about seven at the time, wanted to try. So, she peers into the crystal. "All I see are snowflakes... maybe stars."

Damn.

What follows is some general information about crystal balls. Have fun with it. Experiment. Also, keep the ball away from direct sunlight. Not that it'll harm the crystal, but the thing will act like a magnifying glass and might start a fire.

Originating from ancient cultures such as the Celts and Egyptians, crystal ball scrying involves gazing into a crystal ball or a similar spherical object to access hidden knowledge and receive messages from the spiritual realm. This practice is popular among people who are already familiar with other divination techniques, such as tarot card reading, astrology, and pendulum dowsing.

The crystal ball serves as a portal, amplifying the diviner's psychic abilities and allowing them to perceive images, symbols, and visions that unlock profound insights. It acts as a mirror that reflects one's inner self and the energies surrounding them, making it an invaluable tool for self-reflection and guidance.

To begin your crystal ball scrying journey, it is essential to choose the right crystal ball that resonates with your energy. Common options include clear quartz, amethyst, and obsidian, each possessing unique properties that enhance different aspects of divination.

Cleansing and charging your crystal ball regularly

will ensure its energetic purity and effectiveness. Best practice is to place your crystal ball into a plastic storage bag, then fill it with table salt. No need for expensive sea salts or exotic salt, plain old salt will do the trick. Allow the crystal ball to remain in the salt for at least seven days, then take it out of the salt and charge it for use. I charge all crystals by allowing them to be in direct sunlight for a few minutes. It doesn't take long. Dispose of the salt by flushing it down a toilet or into a sink. Don't take it outside, as the high amount of sodium will harm most plants and animals.

Next up, creating a suitable environment is crucial for successful scrying. Find a quiet and comfortable space where you can concentrate without distractions. Dim the lights and set the mood with candles, incense, or soothing music. Relaxation techniques, such as deep breathing and meditation, can help you enter a focused state of mind. It really needs to be dark around you to prevent stray reflections from obscuring the psychic information you are focusing on.

As you gaze into the crystal ball, allow your mind to relax and be open to receiving messages from the universe. A sign it's beginning to work is seeing what looks like snowflakes swirling in the glass. I figure this is like the old "snow" patterns old TVs picked up with not on a channel. You just haven't gotten onto a potential channel, but keep it up, as getting the static is a good beginning.

Images, symbols, or even words may appear, offering guidance or answers to your queries. Trust your intuition and interpret the messages intuitively, drawing from your knowledge of tarot card reading, astrology, and other divination practices.

Remember, crystal ball scrying is a skill that requires practice and patience. It is a deeply personal experience that can provide profound insights into your life's journey.

Embrace the mysteries of the crystal ball, and let it guide you on your path of self-discovery and spiritual growth.

It's interesting to note - quartz crystals possess a unique structure which allows for the amplification of energy, especially the subtle energy used by psychics. According to legends, the civilization known as Atlantis used crystals to store power and information. Our society does this now. Quartz is a very handy crystal to have around, no matter what form it is in, such as a crystal point or polished ball.

Just make sure the crystal ball you find is actually crystal, and not simply polished glass.

Mirror Scrying

Mirror scrying, also known as catoptromancy, is a

divination technique that has been practiced for centuries by mystics and seers. This ancient art involves gazing into a mirror to perceive hidden insights, future events, or spiritual guidance.

This is one of the methods I can occasionally use with some success. I figure it triggers my remote viewing abilities, then allows me to see images.

For those already familiar with tarot card reading and interpretation, astrology and horoscope analysis, or other divination practices, mirror scrying is a natural next step in expanding your mystical abilities. I'll introduce you to the history, tools, and techniques necessary to embark on this extraordinary journey.

To begin your mirror scrying practice, you will need a mirror specifically designated for divination purposes. Choose a mirror that resonates with you, whether it be a handheld mirror, a scrying mirror, or even a blackened bowl of water. Remember, the mirror serves as a portal to the spirit realm, so it is crucial to cleanse and consecrate it before use. Use salt and charging like with a crystal ball. You can also use an old cast-iron skillet, well-seasoned and almost black, then pour a shallow layer of oil into it.

Once your mirror is prepared, find a quiet and comfortable space where you can focus your attention. The art of mirror scrying requires deep concentration and a calm state of mind. Begin by grounding yourself through meditation or any other relaxation technique that suits you.

When you feel centered, hold the mirror in your hands and gaze upon its surface. Allow your eyes to soften and your vision to blur slightly. As you continue to gaze, you may notice images, symbols, or scenes appearing within the mirror. These visions may come as subtle impressions or vivid pictures. Trust your intuition and let the images guide you.

Interpreting the messages received during mirror scrying is a skill that develops with practice. The diviner's intuition plays a crucial role in deciphering the meaning behind the visions. Pay attention to the emotions, sensations, or thoughts that arise as you gaze into the mirror. These impressions often hold valuable insights and messages from the spiritual realm.

In my experience, I will begin receiving flashes of images, scenes relating to the question I am seeking the answer. I have to open my mind to these images. Then I'll close my eyes and explore the scenes, trying to move the scene around so I can decipher what I am seeing. It's a lot like sitting in a dark theater, and a single frame of film is flashed on the screen, and then it's gone. It also helps to make notes, and when learning to see in a mirror, these notes will help you fathom what the images you saw might mean.

Mirror scrying is a profound divination technique that allows you to tap into the hidden depths of your intuition and connect with the spiritual realm. By mastering this ancient art, you will expand your divinatory abilities and gain valuable insights into the past, present, and future.

Water Scrying

Water scrying stands as one of the most ancient and revered practices. Harnessing the power of water, this technique allows us to tap into the depths of our intuition and unlock hidden truths. With its roots deeply entwined in the history of divination, water scrying is a powerful tool for those who seek to explore the realms of the unknown.

Water scrying, also known as hydromancy, involves gazing into a pool of water to gain insights and answers. As the water acts as a conduit between the physical and spiritual realms, it becomes a mirror for the diviner's subconscious mind. This technique complements other forms of divination, such as tarot card reading, astrology, and pendulum dowsing, enhancing the practitioner's ability to receive accurate and profound messages.

The ancient Greeks used water scrying quite a bit in their temples. Many Greek temples were constructed near natural bodies of water, such as springs, rivers, or pools.

These water sources were considered sacred and believed to be imbued with divine energy. Temples often had special areas designated for divination practices. These areas were designed to create a serene and meditative atmosphere conducive to scrying.

Before scrying, offerings and prayers were made to the deities associated with the temple. The Greeks believed that invoking the blessings of the gods and goddesses would enhance the accuracy of their scrying.

Okay, so to begin your journey into water scrying, find a quiet and undisturbed space where you can immerse yourself in your practice. Choose a bowl or a vessel that resonates with you, filling it with pure water. This can be from a bottle of purified spring water, or from a nearby stream. Take a moment to ground yourself, centering your energy and clearing your mind of any distractions.

As you gaze into the water, allow your vision to soften and your focus to shift. Relax your gaze, letting your eyes rest upon the surface of the water. The ripples and reflections may dance before you, but it is through this fluid medium that the messages from the universe will emerge.

Trust your intuition as images, symbols, and visions begin to form within the water. These messages may come in various forms – shapes, colors, or even moving scenes. Pay attention to the emotions and sensations that arise within you, for they hold the key to unraveling the meaning behind the symbols.

Water scrying is a deeply personal experience, and no two diviners will interpret the messages in the same way. It is essential to develop your own language and understanding of the symbols that appear to you. Keep a journal and record your observations, as this will help you refine your interpretations.

As with any divination practice, patience and practice are key. The more you engage with water scrying, the stronger your connection with the water's energy will become. Through this ancient technique, you will develop a profound understanding of yourself and the world around you.

Fire Scrying

Fire scrying, also known as pyromancy, is a powerful divination technique that has been practiced for centuries. This ancient method involves gazing into flames to receive messages, insights, and visions from the spiritual realm. In the realm of high magic, fire scrying is a revered practice that can provide deep insights into the past, present, and future.

Honestly, this isn't a method I have ever worked with, so this information comes from multiple sources, all summarized here for you. I know I have gazed into a fireplace, or a campfire, and felt myself becoming mesmerized by the sight of the flickering flames. However, during such occasions, I never actually attempted to pull information or seek psychic information with this method.

To engage in fire scrying, one must create a sacred space and ensure a calm and focused mind. It is important to choose a quiet and secluded area where you can safely light a fire. As the flames dance and flicker, they create a mesmerizing spectacle that serves as a portal to the unseen world.

Once the fire is lit, take a few deep breaths and relax your mind and body. Allow yourself to become fully present in the moment and open yourself up to the energies surrounding you. As you gaze into the flames, allow your eyes to soften and your focus to become unfocused. This relaxed state allows your intuition to take over and receive messages from the spiritual realm.

As the fire burns, pay close attention to any shapes, symbols, or patterns that appear in the flames. These images may be subtle or vivid, and they often hold significant meaning. Trust your instincts and let your intuition guide you as you interpret these symbols. The messages received through fire scrying can provide guidance, warnings, or even confirmations of your current path.

Fire scrying is particularly beneficial for people who are already familiar with other divination techniques, such as tarot card reading, astrology, and pendulum dowsing. It complements these practices by offering a different perspective and tapping into the elemental energies of fire. By incorporating fire scrying into your repertoire, you can deepen your connection to the spiritual world and enhance your divination abilities.

Make note, fire scrying requires practice and patience. It is a skill that develops over time, and each session can bring new insights and experiences. Embrace the mystical power of fire and allow it to illuminate your path on the journey of divination. Even if you don't have any luck at first, keep trying.

By gazing into the flames and interpreting the symbols and patterns that arise, practitioners can gain valuable insights and guidance. When combined with other divination practices, fire scrying can deepen one's understanding of the mystical arts and enhance their ability to navigate the complexities of life.

Numerology

Numerology is often used to interpret and harness the power of numbers for various purposes. Here's a summary of the key aspects of numerology in this context:

Numerological Meanings:

Numerologists assign specific meanings to numbers. These meanings can vary depending on the system used, but common interpretations include personality traits, life path, and destiny associated with each number.

Calculating Life Path Number: In magic and the occult, one of the fundamental numerological practices is calculating a person's Life Path Number. This number is derived from their birthdate and is believed to reveal insights into their life's purpose and potential.

Magical Correspondences: Numerology is often used to find correspondences between numbers and other elements of magic, such as colors, herbs, and crystals. These correspondences are used to enhance the effectiveness of rituals and spells.

Timing and Synchronicity: Numerology also plays a role in timing magical activities. Some practitioners believe that certain numbers or numerical patterns are more auspicious for spellwork or rituals. Synchronicities, where specific numbers repeatedly appear in one's life, are considered significant and may guide magical work.

Personal Transformation: Numerology is used as a tool for personal growth and self-discovery. Practitioners may use their numerology charts to gain insight into their strengths, weaknesses, and life challenges, with the aim of improving themselves through magical practices.

Divination: Numerology can be used for divination, much like tarot cards or runes. Numerologists may interpret the significance of numbers drawn or generated randomly to provide guidance and insights into a situation or question.

Other Divination Techniques

In addition to the popular practices of tarot card reading, astrology, and divination techniques like scrying and pendulum dowsing, there is a world of other lesser-known divination techniques that can enhance your knowledge and skills as a divination practitioner. These methods offer unique insights and perspectives into the mysteries of the universe, allowing you to explore the depths of divination further. In this section, we will explore some of these fascinating techniques and their potential applications.

One such technique is palmistry, also known as chiromancy, which involves interpreting the lines and patterns on a person's hand to gain insight into their character traits, potential, and future. By studying the shape of the hand, the lines on the palm, and the mounts, you can unlock a wealth of information about an individual's life path, relationships, and career prospects. Learning palmistry can greatly enhance your ability to provide comprehensive readings and deepen your understanding of human nature.

For those interested in delving into the spiritual realm, automatic writing may be a technique worth exploring. This involves channeling spiritual energy and allowing it to guide your hand as you write. Through automatic writing, you can receive messages from higher beings, spirit guides, or even your own subconscious. It is a powerful method of communication and can provide profound insights and guidance.

In fact, many of my books are written while I'm in a meditative state, and I begin to write after making contact with the gods, goddesses, and other beings I write about. I will often write entire chapters, only to discover what I'd written was different from what I had intended to write. Novelists find this happens when their characters take on a life of their own, and begin a new plot.

Lastly, bibliomancy is a divination technique that involves seeking answers or guidance by randomly selecting and interpreting passages from books, particularly sacred texts or works of literature. By opening a book to a random page and reading the first passage that catches your eye, you can gain valuable insights and messages from the collective wisdom of the written word.

As someone with a passion for tarot card reading, astrology, and divination techniques, exploring these lesser-known methods can broaden your repertoire of skills and deepen your understanding of the ancient art of divination. By incorporating these techniques into your practice, you can offer more varied and insightful readings, providing a more comprehensive experience for your clients. Embrace these other divination techniques and open yourself up to a world of untapped knowledge and wisdom.

Runes

Dating back to the days of the Vikings, runes have intrigued high magic students for centuries. With their unique symbols and intricate meanings, runes offer a fascinating insight into the past, present, and future.

Originating from the Old Norse word "rūna," meaning "secret" or "whisper," runes were traditionally carved into stones, wood, or bone. Each rune carries its own distinct energy and symbolism, making them perfect for those delving into the realms of tarot card reading and interpretation, astrology and horoscope analysis, and various divination techniques and practices.

If you like to work with the tarot, by incorporating runes into your readings can add an extra layer of depth and nuance. By drawing a rune at the beginning of a reading, you can tap into its specific energy and interpret it alongside the tarot cards, enriching your understanding of the situation at hand. Whether it's the protective energy of Algiz or the transformative power of Thurisaz, runes can enhance your ability to provide insightful guidance to those seeking answers.

Astrology enthusiasts will find that runes offer a unique perspective on their birth charts and horoscope analysis. By associating each rune with a particular zodiac sign or planetary influence, one can gain deeper insights into the energies at play in a person's life. The combination of rune symbols and astrological aspects can unlock hidden meanings and shed light on potential pathways for growth and transformation.

Take the time to study and connect with the power of runes. By understanding their symbols, meanings, and associations, you will open yourself to a world of divination possibilities. Let the whispers of the runes guide you as you explore the realms of tarot card reading, astrology, and various divination techniques, allowing you to unlock the secrets of the past, gain clarity in the present, and illuminate the path towards your future.

Ouija Board

Unveiling the Mysteries of Spirit Communication
Nothing can trigger a flame war more than even the

mention of the Ouija Board online. Thing is, it's just a tool, like Tarot or Runes. I mean, if the apocryphal stories are true, then we're dealing with a super paranormal piece of pressed board capable of summoning the dark lords of the underworld. However, none of these fantastic stories are true, they're just out there to give children nightmares.

The Ouija Board, also known as a spirit board or talking board, has captivated the imagination of individuals for decades. It is a flat board marked with letters, numbers, and words, accompanied by a movable planchette. When individuals place their fingertips upon the planchette, it is believed that spirits can guide its movement to spell out messages or answer questions.

While the origins of the Ouija Board remain shrouded in mystery, its use can be traced back to the late 19th century when spiritualism gained popularity. This divination tool quickly became a means to communicate with the spirit realm. However, it is important to approach the Ouija Board with caution and respect, as it can open a gateway to unknown forces. By practicing even the simplest protection statement, one can use the Ouija Board safely.

For tarot card readers and interpreters, the Ouija Board can serve as an additional tool to connect with spirit guides or gain insights into the querent's questions. The board can be used in conjunction with tarot spreads, allowing for a deeper exploration of the energies at play.

Astrology and horoscope enthusiasts may find the Ouija Board a fascinating way to connect with celestial beings or seek guidance from planetary influences. By understanding the planetary correspondences associated with the board, one can align their questions with specific celestial energies.

However, it is crucial to approach the Ouija Board with mindfulness and respect. Before engaging, ensure that you are in a calm and focused state of mind, surrounded by a protective circle or invoking the guidance of benevolent entities. Remember to set clear intentions and establish boundaries to ensure a safe and purposeful exchange.

From preparation rituals and cleansing practices to interpret messages and ensuring ethical conduct, we will guide you through the intricacies of this tool, empowering you to explore the mysteries of spirit communication with confidence and reverence.

Remember, the Ouija Board is a powerful tool that demands respect and responsibility. By approaching it with an open mind and a discerning spirit, you can unlock the potential for profound insights and connections with the unseen realms.

Palmistry

For centuries, palmistry, a fascinating ancient divination technique also known as chiromancy or palm reading, has been practiced. The upcoming section is going to explore the mystical world of palmistry and provide a comprehensive understanding of its origins, methods, and interpretations.

Originating from ancient civilizations such as Mesopotamia, India, and China, palmistry is based on the belief that the lines and shapes on an individual's hands can reveal important insights about their personality traits, life events, and potential future. By analyzing the texture, shape, and lines on the palms, a skilled palm reader can uncover hidden aspects of a person's character and provide guidance on their life path.

Here are the primary lines in palmistry and their accepted indications:

Heart Line: This line curves along the top of the palm, just under the fingers. It is associated with matters of the heart and emotions. A deep, clear line may indicate a passionate and emotionally expressive nature, while a broken or fragmented line could suggest emotional turmoil.

Head Line: Running horizontally just below the heart line, the head line represents one's intellect and thought processes. A long, straight line often indicates a logical and analytical mind, while a wavy line might suggest creativity and imagination.

Life Line: This line arcs around the base of the thumb and encircles the ball of the thumb. Contrary to common belief, it does not predict the length of one's life but is associated with one's vitality and life path. A deep, clear life line may indicate a strong constitution, while a faint or fragmented line could suggest periods of change or uncertainty in life.

Fate Line: Not everyone has a fate line, but it runs vertically from the middle of the palm towards the base. It's associated with one's life path and destiny. A strong, unbroken line might suggest a clear life purpose, while multiple lines or an absent fate line may indicate a more unpredictable journey.

Mounts: These are raised areas at the base of each finger and the center of the palm. They are associated with specific qualities or traits. For example, the mount beneath the index finger (Jupiter mount) is linked to leadership and ambition, while the mount at the base of the thumb (Mars mount) is associated with courage and assertiveness.

You may wish to find a more thorough book on palmistry, so check the list in the appendix under "Suggested Reading".

Tea Leaf Reading

Tea leaf reading, also known as tasseography, is a fascinating divination technique that has been practiced for centuries. In this section, we will delve into the mystical art of tea leaf reading and explore the ancient techniques used to interpret the patterns and symbols left behind in the tea leaves.

For high magic students who are already familiar with tarot card reading and interpretation, astrology and horoscope analysis, as well as other divination techniques and practices, tea leaf reading offers a unique and captivating addition to your repertoire.

Tea leaf reading is a form of divination that involves the interpretation of patterns and symbols formed by tea leaves at the bottom of a cup. It is believed that the energy and essence of the tea leaves transfer onto the water, creating a canvas on which the diviner can read the messages from the spiritual realm. By observing and interpreting these patterns, the practitioner gains insight into the past, present, and future.

Here's a summary of the process:

Preparation:

Choose loose tea leaves or tea bags, preferably with herbal or loose-leaf tea, as they produce more distinct patterns.

Select a plain, preferably white, teacup without any markings or patterns inside.

Brewing the Tea:

Brew your tea as you normally would, focusing on your intention and the question you seek answers to.

Pour the tea into your cup, leaving a small amount of liquid at the bottom. Avoid using a tea strainer to keep the leaves in the cup.

Concentration:

Focus your mind on your question or intention while sipping the tea. Concentrate on the energy and thoughts you wish to infuse into the tea.

Drinking the Tea:

When you've consumed most of the tea, leave a small amount of liquid at the bottom of the cup.

Reading the Leaves:

Hold the cup with your non-dominant hand and rotate it three times in a counterclockwise direction to distribute the leaves.

Interpretation:

Gently tip the cup upside down on a saucer or a cloth to drain any remaining liquid.

Examine the patterns, shapes, and symbols formed by the tea leaves on the cup's interior.

Interpret these patterns intuitively. Some common

symbols include hearts, animals, numbers, or letters. Each symbol may carry a unique meaning or message.

Recording and Analysis:

Take notes or a photograph of the tea leaf patterns for future reference.

Reflect on the symbols and patterns to decipher their significance in relation to your question or intention.

Intuitive Insights:

Trust your intuition to guide your interpretation. In magik, your inner connection to the energies and forces at play is essential.

Practice and Patience:

Like any form of divination, tasseography improves with practice. Over time, you may develop a deeper understanding of the symbols and their meanings.

There are even more methods of Divination I can go into, but this book is growing quite lengthy, so I'll quickly wrap up.

Chapter Thirteen

Putting Divination into Practice

Now it's time to put all this together into something you can actually use. No matter if you are learning, reading for fun, trying to impress friends, or a seasoned occultist and just need to fathom out why a ritual has failed, eventually it's time to begin using one (or more) of these techniques for real. So, how to start?

Creating a Personal Divination Ritual

The art of divination holds a special place in my heart. Whether you are an aspiring tarot card reader, an astrology enthusiast, or someone interested in various divination techniques like scrying or pendulum dowsing, developing a personal divination ritual can enhance your connection to the mystical forces at play. This section will guide you in creating a meaningful and effective ritual that aligns with your individual style and preferences.

Foremost, it is essential to understand that a personal divination ritual is a highly individualized practice. What works for one person may not resonate with another. It is crucial to honor your unique inclinations and instincts throughout this process. For example, I can't get a crystal ball to work, yet I can easily use a scrying mirror.

Begin by finding a sacred space where you feel comfortable and undisturbed. This could be a corner of your room adorned with mystical objects, a secluded spot in nature, or even a dedicated altar. The important thing is that it holds significance for you and allows you to tap into your spiritual energy. My space is a corner of the basement, which can be easily darkened for use with a scrying mirror, or even candle gazing for meditation.

Next, select the divination tool that resonates most with you. This could be a deck of tarot cards, an astrology chart, or any other divination instrument that you feel drawn to. Take the time to understand its symbolism, meanings, and interpretations. Familiarize yourself with its history and the techniques associated with it.

Once you have chosen your tool, incorporate it into your ritual. This could involve cleansing and consecrating it, charging it with your own energy, or even creating a personalized ritual for shuffling or handling the cards. The key is to infuse it with your intentions and make it an extension of your own divinatory abilities.

In addition to your chosen tool, consider incorporating other elements into your ritual. Candles, crystals, incense, and herbs can all contribute to the ambiance and energy of your practice. Experiment with different combinations and observe how they augment your connection to the spiritual realm.

Finally, establish a routine for your personal divination ritual. Consistency is key in developing a deep connection with your divination practice. Set aside a specific time each day or week, depending on your availability, and honor this commitment to yourself and your craft.

Remember, the creation of a personal divination ritual is a journey of self-discovery and spiritual growth. Allow yourself to evolve and adapt as you delve deeper into the mystical arts. Embrace your unique perspective and let it guide you on your path towards divinatory wisdom.

Setting the Intention

Intention is the key to everything in the world of magik, and therefore, setting the intention is a critical step that cannot be overlooked when it comes to successful divination. It doesn't matter if you're a beginner or an expert in the field, comprehending the significance of establishing distinct intentions is crucial to tapping into the potential of age-old divination methods.

Before beginning your divination journey, it is crucial that you take the time to establish a clear intention for your practice. With a clear intention in mind, you can direct your energy and focus towards a specific purpose, allowing it to act as a guiding light. When you set a clearly defined intention, you are effectively forging a powerful connection between your conscious and subconscious mind, which in turn allows you to access the immense reserves of divine wisdom at your disposal.

For tarot card reading and interpretation, setting the intention enables you to attune your mind to the cards' symbolic language. By clearly stating your purpose, whether it is seeking guidance, gaining insight, or finding clarity, you align your thoughts and emotions with the cards, allowing their messages to resonate deeply within you.

Similarly, in astrology and horoscope analysis, setting the intention directs your attention to specific aspects of a birth chart or celestial event. By focusing on what you aim to uncover or understand, you open the gateway to interpreting the cosmic patterns and their influence on individuals' lives.

Divination techniques like scrying and pendulum

dowsing also benefit from setting intentions. By defining your objective, you create a sacred space within yourself and the environment, enhancing your receptivity to the subtle energies surrounding you. This heightened awareness increases your ability to perceive and interpret the signs and symbols that arise during these practices.

Older, more archaic rituals to so-called demons used black mirror scrying as a way to communicate with the demonic forces being called.

To set a powerful intention, take a moment to center yourself. Clear your mind of distractions, ground yourself in the present moment, and visualize your desired outcome. Speak your intention aloud, infusing it with conviction and emotion. Allow yourself to embrace the intention fully, surrendering any doubts or uncertainties.

Remember, the intention you set is the driving force behind your divination practice. It is the compass that guides you through the labyrinth of symbolism and ancient wisdom.

As you delve deeper into the mystical arts, never underestimate the transformative power of setting clear intentions. With each practice, refine and strengthen your intentions, and witness how your divination abilities flourish and evolve.

Clearing and Protecting the Space

Let's take a brief look into the essential practices and techniques to create a sacred environment for your divination sessions. As an occultist or student of magik, you understand the importance of setting the right atmosphere to establish a strong connection with the spiritual realm. Whether you are a Tarot card reader, astrologer, or practitioner of various divination techniques, this chapter is tailored specifically to your needs.

Clearing the space is the first step in preparing for any divination session. It helps remove any negative or stagnant energies, ensuring a clean slate for your work. Begin by physically cleaning the area, tidying up and organizing your tools. Then, consider using smudging techniques with pure incense resin to purify the space. Visualize the smoke dispersing any unwanted energies, leaving behind a fresh and inviting atmosphere.

I avoid using sage, as it's fine if you wish to enjoy the aroma of a campfire, but it does little in actually clearing a space of negative energies. I use pure frankincense, and this has worked for me in the many decades of sanctifying my space for any work.

Next, let's focus on protection. Shielding yourself and the space from any unwanted influences is crucial during divination. Start by creating a protective boundary around your workspace using visualization or physical objects. This can be done by envisioning a shimmering golden energy field surrounding you or placing protective crystals such as black tourmaline or amethyst around the area.

In addition to these general practices, it's important to tailor your clearing and protection techniques to your specific divination niche. For Tarot card readers, consider consecrating your deck by dedicating it to the divine and asking for its guidance.

Astrologers may find it helpful to incorporate planetary symbols or invoke the support of specific celestial beings. Those practicing divination techniques like scrying or pendulum dowsing can benefit from creating a sacred ritual or using consecrated tools to enhance their connection.

Remember, these practices are not mere superstition; they serve as a foundation for your work. Clearing and protecting the space ensures that you can access higher realms of consciousness and information without distractions or interference. By incorporating these techniques regularly, you will develop a sacred space where your intuition can flourish, and divination becomes a powerful tool for self-discovery and guidance.

Choosing the Right Tools

As someone delving into the fascinating world of divination, perhaps for the first time, one of the most crucial aspects of your journey is selecting the right tools. The tools you choose can greatly impact the accuracy and effectiveness of your readings, as well as enhance your connection with the spiritual realm. In this section, we will explore the essential tools for three popular niches in divination: Tarot card reading and interpretation, astrology and horoscope analysis, and various divination techniques and practices.

Tarot Card Reading and Interpretation: The tarot deck is a powerful tool that allows the diviner to gain insights into the past, present, and future. When choosing a tarot deck, it is essential to find one that resonates with your energy and intuition. There are countless designs and interpretations available, ranging from traditional Rider-Waite decks to more modern and artistic ones. Take the time to explore different decks and select the one that speaks to you on a personal level.

Additionally, consider investing in books or online resources that provide in-depth interpretations and meanings for each card, enabling you to develop your skills as a tarot reader. I strongly suggested only one book, Power Tarot.

More details about this book are in the appendix.

Astrology and Horoscope Analysis: Astrology is a complex and ancient art that requires a deep understanding of celestial bodies and their influence on human lives. To begin your journey in astrology, you can find an ephemeris, a book or table that contains the positions of celestial bodies at specific times, or a well-rounded computer program which will give you all the tools you will need. Good software can aid you in calculating birth charts and interpreting planetary movements.

Divination Techniques and Practices: Scrying, pendulum dowsing, and other divination techniques require specific tools tailored to each practice. For scrying, a black mirror or crystal ball is commonly used, while pendulum dowsing requires a pendulum made of a material that resonates with you, such as crystal or metal. Other divination practices may require items such as runes, tea leaves, or even playing cards. Experiment with different tools to find the ones that complement your energy and allow you to connect with the spiritual realm more effectively.

Remember, the tools you choose are extensions of your energy and intuition. They should feel comfortable and resonate with your unique spiritual journey. Take the time to explore and experiment with different options until you find the tools that enhance your divination practice and deepen your connection to the ancient art of divination.

Performing the Divination

You can use a small table near your space for divination. Sometimes, I'll shuffle and work a reading while at my computer desk, or even spread the cards out on my bed, or any handy flat surface. In my experience, as soon as I begin to draw cards, I'll start picking up information about the question or client I am reading. I often use the tarot to clarify what I've already seen using scrying or the pendulum.

Tarot card reading and interpretation is one of the most popular and widely practiced forms of divination. There are cards for every subject, including popular culture and specific ancient deities. To perform a Tarot reading, shuffle the deck while focusing on your question or the situation at hand. Then, draw cards and interpret their meanings in relation to your query. Remember, intuition plays a crucial role in Tarot readings, so trust your instincts and let the cards speak to you.

Astrology and horoscope analysis is another ancient divination technique that has stood the test of time. By studying the positions and movements of celestial bodies, astrologers can gain insights into an individual's personality traits, strengths, weaknesses, and even future events. To perform astrological divination, you need to calculate birth charts, analyze planetary aspects, and interpret their influence on different areas of life. By understanding the energies at play, you can guide others towards self-discovery and empowerment.

Divination techniques and practices, such as scrying and pendulum dowsing, offer additional tools for exploring the unknown. You can even use a deck of regular playing cards to access hidden knowledge and receive visions. Pendulum dowsing, on the other hand, employs a weighted object suspended from a string or chain to answer yes or no questions. These techniques tap into your subconscious mind and the collective unconscious, allowing you to access information beyond the limitations of your ordinary senses.

Regardless of the divination technique you choose, it is essential to create a sacred space and cultivate a focused mindset. Clear your mind of distractions, ground yourself, and connect with your spiritual guides or higher self. Divination is a sacred act and should be treated with reverence and respect.

These divination techniques require a lot of practice, with you working test readings on the people around you, or in groups on social media. The more you work with these techniques, the more your intuition will sharpen, and the deeper your connection to the mystical realm will become. Embrace the mysteries that lie ahead and embark on this transformative journey of self- discovery and enlightenment.

Reflecting on the Results

By now, you may have decided on which divination techniques you wish to master. Now, it is time to reflect on the results of your practice and gather valuable insights.

Reflecting on the results of your divination sessions is crucial to deepen your understanding and enhance your skills. It allows you to connect the dots, identify patterns, and gain new perspectives on the messages received from the divine.

Remember, at all times, the energy of a reading could shift, causing a different outcome. Always remind your clients of this, and that if a bad outcome is seen, that outcome can be shifted by taking corrective actions. A reading is a snapshot of the energies at the time of the reading.

When it comes to tarot card reading and interpretation, reflecting on the results is essential to uncover the hidden meanings behind the cards. Take the time to journal your readings, contemplating the symbols, imagery, and emotions evoked by each card. Look for recurring themes or symbols across multiple readings to gain a deeper understanding of their significance. By reflecting on the results, you can develop a personal connection with your tarot deck and refine your intuition.

Astrology and horoscope analysis also require thoughtful reflection. As you observe the planetary movements and their impact on individuals' lives, take note of the patterns that emerge. Reflect on the accuracy of your predictions and the insights gained from studying birth charts. Consider the nuances and complexities of each astrological aspect, allowing yourself to grow in confidence and accuracy as an astrologer.

For those who have explored divination techniques like scrying or pendulum dowsing, reflecting on the results provides a gateway into the realm of symbolism and subconscious communication. Analyze the images or messages received during scrying sessions, noting any recurring symbols or themes.

Reflect on the accuracy of your pendulum dowsing predictions and consider the factors that may have influenced the outcomes.

Remember, reflection is not limited to analyzing the results alone; it is also an opportunity for personal growth. As you reflect on your divination practices, acknowledge your strengths and areas for improvement.

Ethical Considerations in Divination

As practitioners of tarot card reading and interpretation, astrology and horoscope analysis, and other divination techniques, we have a responsibility to approach our craft with integrity, respect, and compassion. This section explores the ethical guidelines that should guide us as we navigate the mystical realms of divination.

First and foremost, it is essential to recognize the power and influence we hold as diviners. Our clients come to us seeking guidance, insight, and clarity. It is imperative to approach each reading with empathy and a genuine desire to help. We should always prioritize the well-being and autonomy of our clients, presenting them with information in an empowering manner rather than dictating their choices or manipulating their beliefs.

Another crucial ethical consideration is maintaining confidentiality. Clients often share personal and sensitive information during divination sessions. As psychics, we must respect their privacy and ensure that their trust is upheld. This means not discussing or disclosing any details of their reading without their explicit permission.

Furthermore, diviners should be aware of their limitations and be honest about what they can and cannot provide. It is important to set realistic expectations with clients and refrain from making definitive predictions or claims that cannot be substantiated. We should always emphasize that divination is a tool for guidance, not an absolute oracle of the future.

When working a reading, we might be asked to look at someone else, and this usually places us in a bad spot. It's unethical to perform a reading of someone without their knowledge or permission. When this happens, and I have encountered this a lot of time in my past practice in doing readings, the information you will get will be filtered through the mind of the person asking for the reading. You'll see that other person via filters which will mask the reality.

In addition to client-centered ethics, we must also consider the ethical implications of our own practices. It is crucial to approach divination with a clear and centered mind, free from personal biases or influences that may cloud our readings. We should continuously strive to enhance our skills through study, practice, and self-reflection, ensuring that we are providing the most accurate and unbiased readings possible.

In conclusion, ethical considerations are of utmost importance in the practice of divination. As divination practitioner specializing in tarot card reading, astrology, and other divination techniques, it is our duty to approach our craft with integrity, respect, and compassion. By adhering to ethical guidelines, we can ensure that our divination sessions are empowering, confidential, and culturally sensitive, providing our clients with the guidance they seek while upholding the sacredness of this ancient art.

Respect for Free Will

It is crucial for us to understand and uphold the principle of respect for free will.

This fundamental belief underpins the ethics and integrity of all divination practices, including tarot card reading and interpretation, astrology and horoscope analysis, as well as various divination techniques and practices like scrying and pendulum dowsing. As aspiring diviners, it is essential to recognize and honor the autonomy and free choices of individuals when delving into their destinies.

Tarot card reading and interpretation, a popular and intricate divination art, relies heavily on the concept of free will. Each tarot card represents different aspects of life and potential outcomes. However, it is crucial to remember that the cards themselves do not determine a person's fate. Instead, they offer guidance and insights into the possible paths that lie ahead. Respect for free will means recognizing that individuals possess the power to shape their own lives, and the tarot serves as a tool to assist them in making informed decisions.

It's also important to understand if the same cards continue to appear in a tarot reading, either for a client, friend, or even yourself, you need to pay careful attention to this card. Make a note, and track how many times the message repeats. The tarot will do this. Sometimes, the cards will emphasize a specific outcome, and it is up to us to determine what the message might be.

Similarly, astrology and horoscope analysis also adhere to the principle of respect for free will. Astrologers study the positions of celestial bodies at the time of a person's birth to gain insights into their personality traits, potential challenges, and opportunities. However, astrology does not dictate a person's actions or choices. It merely provides a cosmic roadmap, allowing individuals to navigate their lives with self-awareness and a deeper understanding of their unique cosmic blueprint.

Divination techniques and practices like scrying and pendulum dowsing also require a deep respect for free will. Scrying, the ancient art of gazing into reflective surfaces or objects, allows diviners to tap into their intuition and interpret symbols and images. Pendulum dowsing, on the other hand, involves using a pendulum to seek answers to specific questions. Respect for free will in these practices means understanding that the information received is not absolute and should always be approached with open-mindedness and sensitivity towards the individual's choices and decisions.

In conclusion, the principle of respect for free will is the guiding light for all high magic students, especially those specializing in tarot card reading and interpretation, astrology and horoscope analysis, as well as various divination techniques and practices.

Upholding this principle is crucial for maintaining the ethical and moral foundation of divination arts. By embracing the concept of free will, diviners empower individuals to take charge of their own destiny, offering guidance and insights without imposing or manipulating their choices. Remember, as students of the mystical arts, it is our duty to honor and respect the autonomy and free will of all those who seek our guidance.

Chapter Fourteen

Tarot Quick Reference

Major Arcana

Here's a brief overview of each card's meaning:

The Fool: Beginnings, spontaneity, new adventures.

The Magician: Skill, creativity, manifestation.

The High Priestess: Intuition, hidden knowledge, mysteries.

The Empress: Nurturing, abundance, fertility.

The Emperor: Authority, structure, control.

The Hierophant: Tradition, spirituality, guidance.

The Lovers: Relationships, choices, harmony.

The Chariot: Willpower, determination, overcoming obstacles.

The Hermit: Reflection, solitude, inner guidance.

Wheel of Fortune: Change, cycles, fate.

Justice: Fairness, balance, ethical decisions.

The Hanged Man: Surrender, new perspectives, sacrifice.

Death: Transformation, letting go, rebirth.

Temperance: Balance, moderation, harmony.

The Devil: Temptation, materialism, bondage.

The Tower: Sudden change, upheaval, revelation.

The Star: Hope, inspiration, spiritual guidance.

The Moon: Illusion, subconscious, intuition.

The Sun: Success, vitality, happiness.

Judgment: Reckoning, self-reflection, transformation.

The World: Completion, fulfillment, integration.

These summaries provide a basic understanding of the meanings associated with each Major Arcana card.

Wands:

Ace of Wands: The Ace of Wands represents new beginnings, inspiration, and the spark of a creative or passionate idea. It signifies the birth of a new project, adventure, or venture that holds great potential.

Two of Wands: The Two of Wands represents the need to make decisions and take the first steps toward manifesting your visions. It suggests balance between planning and action, as you explore possibilities and set your intentions.

Three of Wands: This card signifies expansion,

progress, and foresight. It indicates that your initial efforts are starting to bear fruit and that you're seeing the results of your actions. It's a card of anticipation and looking ahead to future opportunities.

Four of Wands: The Four of Wands represents celebration, harmony, and joyful events. It often indicates a time of achievement, happiness, and the coming together of people to share in a sense of accomplishment.

Five of Wands: This card reflects challenges, conflicts, and competition. It suggests that there might be disagreements or differing opinions, but these conflicts can also lead to growth and the emergence of creative solutions.

Six of Wands: The Six of Wands symbolizes victory, recognition, and public acclaim. It signifies a successful outcome and a sense of achievement that comes from your efforts being acknowledged by others.

Seven of Wands: This card represents standing your ground, defending your beliefs, and overcoming obstacles. It's a symbol of resilience, courage, and the determination to protect what you've worked hard to achieve.

Eight of Wands: The Eight of Wands signifies swift movement, progress, and messages coming in quickly. It suggests that things are moving forward rapidly, and you might need to adapt to changes or new developments.

Nine of Wands: This card symbolizes resilience,

determination, and the strength to persevere through challenges. It suggests that you've come a long way and have the inner resources to keep going despite setbacks.

Ten of Wands: The Ten of Wands represents burdens, responsibilities, and the need to lighten your load. It suggests that you might be taking on too much or carrying the weight of others' expectations, and it's time to find a better balance.

Wands Court Cards:

Page of Wands: Curiosity, exploration, and youthful enthusiasm.

Knight of Wands: Action, adventure, and a bold approach to life.

Queen of Wands: Confidence, leadership, and a strong, nurturing presence.

King of Wands: Visionary leadership, creativity, and taking charge of situations.

Cups:

Ace of Cups: Emotional new beginnings, love, intuition.

Two of Cups: Connection, partnership, mutual attraction.

Three of Cups: Celebration, friendship, social

gatherings.

Four of Cups: Contemplation, introspection, reevaluation.

Five of Cups: Loss, disappointment, grief.

Six of Cups: Nostalgia, childhood memories, giving.

Seven of Cups: Choices, dreams, illusions.

Eight of Cups: Walking away, seeking something more meaningful.

Nine of Cups: Contentment, wishes fulfilled, emotional satisfaction.

Ten of Cups: Harmony, family, emotional fulfillment.

Ace of Cups: The Ace of Cups is the chalice of pure emotion and intuition, overflowing with potential for deep connections and spiritual experiences. As an expert in occult literature, you understand that this card represents the wellspring of the heart, offering you the chance to tap into your emotions and connect with the divine. It encourages you to embrace and channel your feelings in your magical work and writings.

Two of Cups: The Two of Cups symbolizes partnerships and connections, both romantic and spiritual. It's a reflection of harmony between your inner and outer worlds. Just as your occult knowledge allows you to decipher hidden truths, this card's energy invites you to explore the intricate dance of connections between individuals and their spiritual journeys.

Three of Cups: The Three of Cups is a joyful celebration of community, friendship, and shared experiences. Your understanding of magical practices can enhance your ability to create meaningful rituals that honor these connections. This card encourages you to embrace the power of togetherness in your magical work.

Four of Cups: The Four of Cups speaks to contemplation and introspection. Just as you delve into the depths of occult mysteries, this card suggests that you seek meaning beyond the surface. It encourages you to explore your emotional landscape and consider new perspectives that can enrich your magical understanding.

Five of Cups: This card embodies a sense of loss and disappointment. As you navigate the intricacies of the mystical, you recognize that challenges are often pathways to growth. The Five of Cups invites you to acknowledge your emotions, learn from setbacks, and use them as catalysts for transformation.

Six of Cups: The Six of Cups is a card of nostalgia, innocence, and reconnecting with the past. Your expertise in the occult allows you to appreciate the layers of symbolism and meaning in this card. It encourages you to honor your roots, draw inspiration from ancient wisdom, and weave it into your present magical practices.

Seven of Cups: The Seven of Cups reveals a world of dreams and choices. Just as your occult literature explores the diverse tapestry of magical paths, this card reminds you to discern your true desires amidst the myriad options. It encourages you to connect with your intuition and focus your intentions.

Eight of Cups: The Eight of Cups signifies a journey of emotional and spiritual exploration. Your affinity for occult knowledge allows you to understand the transformative power of leaving behind what no longer serves you. This card encourages you to embark on a quest for deeper understanding and fulfillment.

Nine of Cups: Known as the "Wish Card," the Nine of Cups symbolizes emotional contentment and fulfillment. Your connection to mystical forces enhances your ability to manifest your desires through intention and alignment. This card encourages you to tap into your intuitive powers and create your own reality.

Ten of Cups: The Ten of Cups represents harmony, joy, and emotional abundance. Just as your magical practices bring you closer to universal truths, this card reflects a deep sense of spiritual connection. It encourages you to cultivate relationships and experiences that bring lasting happiness and fulfillment.

Cups Court Cards:

Page of Cups: The Page embodies sensitivity and creative potential. Your expertise in the occult allows you to channel your intuitive insights into artistic and magical expressions.

Knight of Cups: The Knight's romantic and imaginative energy resonates with your affinity for magical and mystical realms. Your understanding of symbolism can guide you as you seek to balance your passions with spiritual pursuits.

Queen of Cups: The Queen's nurturing and intuitive presence mirrors your own deep connection to the emotional and spiritual. Just as she listens to her heart, you can draw on your occult wisdom to provide compassionate guidance to others.

King of Cups: The King's emotional mastery aligns with your understanding of the intricate interplay between the mundane and the magical. Your expertise allows you to navigate your emotions and connect with others on a profound level.

Swords:

Ace of Swords: Mental clarity, truth, breakthroughs.

Two of Swords: Indecision, choices, stalemate.

Three of Swords: Heartbreak, pain, sorrow. (Can

also mean physical heart issues)

Four of Swords: Rest, recuperation, contemplation.

Five of Swords: Conflict, manipulation, defeat.

Six of Swords: Transition, moving on, finding a better place.

Seven of Swords: Deception, stealth, trickery.

Eight of Swords: Restriction, feeling trapped, self-imposed limitations.

Nine of Swords: Anxiety, fear, nightmares.

Ten of Swords: Rock bottom, betrayal, a painful ending.

Ace of Swords: The Ace of Swords represents the birth of a new idea, a surge of mental clarity, and the potential for breakthroughs. As an expert in occult literature, you understand that this card embodies the power of the intellect to cut through illusions and reveal truths. It invites you to channel this mental energy into your magical work and writings, using your insights to shape your reality.

Two of Swords: The Two of Swords speaks to decisions and balance. Just as you navigate the intricate symbolism of the occult, this card encourages you to find harmony between opposing thoughts and ideas. It suggests that your ability to discern hidden meanings can guide you toward making informed choices.

Three of Swords: The Three of Swords represents heartache and emotional pain. Your understanding of the occult teaches you that pain is often a catalyst for growth and transformation. This card invites you to delve into the depths of your emotions, using your insights to heal and mend your inner world. It can also mean physical heart problems. (I kept getting this card, then I had a literal heart attack followed by surgery, so pay attention!)

Four of Swords: The Four of Swords signifies rest and introspection. As someone deeply connected to the mystical, you recognize the importance of retreat and reflection. This card encourages you to harness the power of stillness to recharge your mind and gather your thoughts.

Five of Swords: This card reflects conflict and tension. Just as you unravel hidden meanings in your studies, the Five of Swords suggests that understanding others' perspectives can lead to resolution. It encourages you to approach challenges with a mind open to diverse viewpoints.

Six of Swords: The Six of Swords symbolizes transition and moving forward. Your connection to the mystical allows you to see the bigger picture and embrace change as a natural part of the journey. This card invites you to navigate transitions with the wisdom gained from your occult studies.

Seven of Swords: The Seven of Swords speaks of deception and stealth. Your understanding of the esoteric can aid you in uncovering hidden motives and truths. This card encourages you to trust your intuition and be aware of potential illusions, both in your magical work and in everyday situations.

Eight of Swords: The Eight of Swords represents feeling trapped or restricted. Your insights into hidden realms can guide you in finding solutions to perceived limitations. This card encourages you to use your intellectual prowess to free yourself from mental constraints.

Nine of Swords: This card embodies anxiety and worry. Just as you seek to uncover hidden knowledge, the Nine of Swords invites you to confront your fears and address the underlying causes of your mental distress. It encourages you to use your understanding of the mind to find peace.

Ten of Swords: The Ten of Swords signifies an ending or a difficult culmination. Your connection to the mystical allows you to perceive the transformative potential even in challenging moments. This card invites you to let go of what no longer serves you and embrace the rebirth that follows.

Swords Court Cards:

Page of Swords: The Page embodies youthful

curiosity and intellectual exploration. Your expertise in the occult allows you to channel your inquisitiveness into your magical practices and understanding of hidden truths.

Knight of Swords: The Knight's assertive energy resonates with your determination to unveil secrets and mysteries. Your knowledge can guide you as you charge forward in pursuit of both intellectual and magical quests.

Queen of Swords: The Queen's wisdom and analytical mind mirror your own affinity for unraveling complex ideas. Just as she seeks truth and clarity, you can use your occult knowledge to guide others toward deeper understanding.

King of Swords: The King's authoritative presence aligns with your understanding of the power of thought and communication. Your expertise allows you to wield your intellectual prowess to lead and guide others on their paths of discovery.

Pentacles:

Ace of Pentacles: Material opportunities, new beginnings, prosperity.

Two of Pentacles: Balance, adaptability, juggling responsibilities.

Three of Pentacles: Collaboration, teamwork, skill development.

Four of Pentacles: Security, possessiveness, financial

stability.

Five of Pentacles: Hardship, poverty, feeling left out.

Six of Pentacles: Generosity, charity, receiving help.

Seven of Pentacles: Patience, investment, waiting for results.

Eight of Pentacles: Dedication, craftsmanship, honing skills.

Nine of Pentacles: Luxury, self-sufficiency, enjoying the fruits of labor.

Ten of Pentacles: Wealth, legacy, family abundance.

Ace of Pentacles: The Ace of Pentacles represents the seed of material and physical manifestation. Just as your occult studies delve into the hidden aspects of reality, this card encourages you to ground your mystical insights in practical endeavors. It invites you to channel your energy into projects that have the potential to flourish and bring tangible results.

Two of Pentacles: The Two of Pentacles signifies balance and adaptability. As you navigate the complexities of occult symbolism, this card encourages you to find harmony between your spiritual pursuits and practical responsibilities. It suggests that your ability to juggle diverse aspects of life can lead to stability.

Three of Pentacles: The Three of Pentacles

symbolizes collaboration and craftsmanship. Your understanding of mystical forces allows you to appreciate the beauty of intricate details. This card encourages you to combine your occult knowledge with practical skills to create something of lasting value.

Four of Pentacles: The Four of Pentacles speaks of security and holding onto resources. Your expertise in the occult enables you to understand the balance between abundance and attachment. This card invites you to assess your relationship with material possessions and seek a sense of security that goes beyond the physical.

Five of Pentacles: This card embodies challenges and hardship. Just as you explore hidden wisdom, the Five of Pentacles reminds you that difficulties can lead to resilience and growth. It encourages you to seek support when needed and use your practical skills to overcome setbacks.

Six of Pentacles: The Six of Pentacles represents generosity and sharing. Your connection to the mystical allows you to appreciate the interconnectedness of all things. This card encourages you to use your resources to support others and foster a sense of community.

Seven of Pentacles: The Seven of Pentacles signifies assessment and patience. Your understanding of the hidden aspects of life allows you to recognize the value of delayed gratification. This card invites you to reflect on your progress and make adjustments to ensure long-term success.

Eight of Pentacles: The Eight of Pentacles symbolizes craftsmanship and dedication. Just as you delve into the intricacies of the occult, this card suggests that your commitment to mastering your craft can lead to mastery in both practical and mystical pursuits.

Nine of Pentacles: This card embodies independence and self-sufficiency. Your affinity for occult knowledge allows you to find abundance within yourself. The Nine of Pentacles encourages you to celebrate your achievements and enjoy the fruits of your labor.

Ten of Pentacles: The Ten of Pentacles signifies wealth and legacy. Your connection to the mystical world gives you insights into the broader significance of material abundance. This card invites you to create a stable foundation that supports not only your own well-being but also the well-being of generations to come.

Pentacles Court Cards:

Page of Pentacles: The Page embodies curiosity and a desire for practical learning. Your expertise in the occult can guide you as you explore new areas of knowledge and translate your insights into tangible skills.

Knight of Pentacles: The Knight's steady and practical energy aligns with your ability to apply mystical insights in a grounded manner. Your knowledge allows you to approach tasks with determination and a methodical approach.

Queen of Pentacles: The Queen's nurturing presence reflects your understanding of the interconnectedness of all things. Just as she cares for her realm, you can use your mystical insights to create a harmonious and abundant environment.

King of Pentacles: The King's mastery of the material world resonates with your practical knowledge and understanding of mystical forces. Your expertise allows you to navigate both realms with wisdom and authority.

Appendix

Suggested Reading

Power Tarot by Trish Macgregor and Phyllis Vega
ISBN: 978-0684841854 *(THE best book on tarot of all the ones I've owned)*

"The Tarot Bible: The Definitive Guide to the Cards and Spreads," by Sarah Bartlett

"The Only Tarot Book You'll Ever Need: Interpret the Cards That Hold Your Future," by Skye Alexander

"The Crystal Bible," by Judy Hall

"Pendulum Magic for Beginners: Tap Into Your Inner Wisdom," by Richard Webster

"The Complete Book of Numerology," by David A. Phillips

"Runes: Reading the Past," by Kim Farnell

"Tea Leaf Reading: A Practical Guide," by Caroline Dow

"The Book of Thoth: A Short Essay on the Tarot of the Egyptians," by Aleister Crowley

"The I Ching or Book of Changes," translated by Richard Wilhelm

"The Complete Book of Palmistry" by Joyce Wilson

"Palmistry: Apprentice to Pro in 24 Hours; The Easiest Palmistry Course Ever Written" by Johnny Fincham

"The Art of Palmistry" by Anna Southgate

"The Encyclopedia of Palmistry" by Edward D. Campbell

"Palm Reading for Beginners: Find Your Future in the Palm of Your Hand" by Richard Webster

Glossary of Terms

As students of high magik, it is essential to familiarize yourselves with the terminology and concepts used in the realm of pendulum divination. This glossary aims to provide you with a comprehensive list of terms that will help you navigate the mystical world of divination.

Arcana: The two main divisions of the tarot deck, the Major Arcana and the Minor Arcana, representing the spiritual and practical aspects of life, respectively.

Archetype: Universal symbols or patterns that resonate with the collective unconscious, enabling deeper interpretation and connection with the cards.

Aura: The energy field surrounding all living beings. Pendulum practitioners often learn to sense and interpret the colors and vibrations of auras.

Chakras: The seven energy centers in the body that correspond to different aspects of human life. Balancing and aligning the chakras is often a part of pendulum work.

Clearing: The process of removing negative or stagnant energy from oneself, an object, or a space. Pendulum clearing techniques are employed to restore balance and harmony.

Court Cards: The Tarot cards representing people or personalities, including the Kings, Queens, Knights, and Pages.

Divination: The practice of seeking insight or knowledge of the unknown through various spiritual methods, such as the pendulum, tarot cards, or scrying.

Dowsing: The act of using a pendulum to locate underground water, minerals, or objects by tapping into the Earth's energy.

Elemental Associations: The four elements— Fire, Water, Air, and Earth—associated with the suits of the Minor Arcana, providing additional layers of interpretation.

Energy: The life force that flows through all living beings and objects. In pendulum divination, understanding and harnessing different energy frequencies is crucial.

Grids: Patterns or layouts formed by placing crystals or other sacred objects in a specific arrangement to enhance the energy flow during pendulum work.

Intuition: The ability to understand or know something instinctively without the need for conscious reasoning. The pendulum helps to amplify and interpret intuitive messages.

Major Arcana: The 22 cards that hold significant spiritual and transformative messages, representing major life events and archetypal energies.

Minor Arcana: Comprising 56 cards divided into four suits—Wands, Cups, Swords, and Pentacles—representing everyday events and challenges.

Pendulum: A weighted object, often a crystal or metal, suspended on a chain or string, used to receive intuitive guidance by tapping into the energy of the divine.

Programming: The process of imprinting specific intentions or questions onto the pendulum. This enables it to provide accurate guidance and answers.

Protection: The act of creating a safe and sacred space before engaging in pendulum divination. This ensures that only positive energies are present during the session.

Reversed Cards: Tarot cards that appear upside down, indicating a reversed or blocked energy in the reading and requiring careful consideration during interpretation.

Scrying: A method of divination that involves gazing into a reflective or translucent surface, such as a crystal ball or mirror, to receive insights and visions.

Significator: A card intentionally chosen to represent the seeker or the subject of the reading, providing a focal point for interpretation.

Spirit Guides: Non-physical beings who assist and guide us on our spiritual journeys. The pendulum can be used to communicate with these guides and receive their wisdom.

Spreads: Different layouts of the cards on the table, each with its own purpose and structure. Examples include the Celtic Cross, Three-Card Spread, and the Horseshoe Spread.

Subconscious Mind: The part of the mind that operates below the level of conscious awareness and can be accessed through pendulum divination to reveal hidden truths and insights.

Symbolism: The rich imagery and symbols depicted on each tarot card, carrying profound meaning and allowing for intuitive interpretation.

Tarot Deck: The complete set of 78 cards, including the Major and Minor Arcana, each with its unique symbolism and energy.

Trump Cards: Another term for the Major Arcana cards, often associated with significant life lessons and transformative experiences.

Yes/No Responses: The basic form of communication between the pendulum and the diviner. Establishing clear signals for yes and no is crucial for accurate divination.

About the Author

Dave is an author of adult fantasy (The Furies series) as well as author of occult books about magick.

David began working ritual magick back in the 1970s. He took a brief break, then used the power of this magick to create a photography career which took him to Los Angeles and work as a photographer for multiple magazines.

David has studied magick in all forms, and in 2018, released a three-part magick instruction course in High Magick. Thousands of students have benefited from David's unique teaching style, making ceremonial magick accessible to everyone.

This book on Divination is the eleventh book in his High Magik series.

Dave also has a series Grecian Magick, exploring the

aspects of ceremonial magick with the gods and goddesses of ancient Greece.

Dave's Facebook Page:
https://www.facebook.com/DavePsychic/

Secrets of Magick Facebook Group:
https://www.facebook.com/groups/secretsofmagick

Dave's webpage, book readings and his services:
https://davepsychic.com
Then his e-learning website for magik classes
https://highmagikacademy.com

Magick Books by David Thompson
Available on EPUB, Paperback and Hardcover.

<u>High Magick Series</u>
- High Magick 101
- Daemons of High Magick
- Daemons and the Law of Attraction
- Magick of Astaroth
- Lilith: Goddess of Darkness and Light
- High Magick Workbook (paperback only)

High Magick supplemental material

- Tarot Reading Logbook (Paperback only)
- Tarot Journal: Power of the Tarot (Paperback Only)
- Book of Shadows: A Personal Grimoire (Paperback only)

Grecian Magick Series

- Magick of Apollo
- Magick of Hermes
- Magick of Aphrodite
- Magick of Fortuna
- Greco-Roman Wealth Magick
- Magick of the Sirens/Magick of the Muses

Fiction Novels by David Thompson

The Furies Series

- Angels of Vengeance
- Descent into Tartarus
- Furies: Beginnings
- Brianna: Making of a Fury

To subscribe to Dave's mailing list, for new book announcements, and class announcements, scan his code and fill in the form!

Pendulum Supplemental Material

Letter to Robin – the source for the best general purpose Pendulum dowsing chart ever made.

https://lettertorobin.files.wordpress.com/2016/06/rbn_10_4_english.pdf

Basic Pendulum Charts

Alphabet Chart

Yes/No and Write your own answers

Write in your own answers

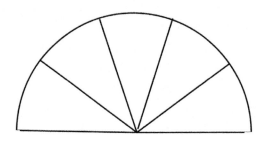

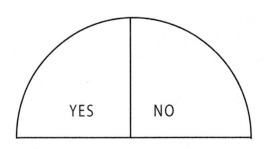

Calendar Chart

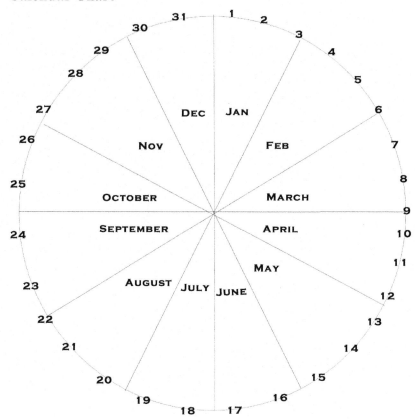

Full sized charts can be found on my website at

https://davepsychic.com/pendulum-charts/

Printed in Great Britain
by Amazon

28470931R00155